Love Like a God

Transform Your Relationship and Elevate Shadow Work

A Couples Therapy Guide for Healing Emotional Wounds and Inner Childhood Traumas, to Build Lasting Bonds Through Personal Growth.

Monica Roy

Copyright © 2024 by Monica Roy.

All rights reserved. No portion of this book may be reproduced mechanically, electronically, or by any other means, including photocopying without written permission of the publisher.

Table of Contents

Introduction 4
   Gods and Goddesses: The Dynamics in Romantic Relationships 6

Chapter 1. Exploring the Goddesses. The Divine Feminine Energies 8
   The Goddess Who Lives in You 8
   Ancestral Energies and Relationships 9
   Aphrodite (The Lover) 10
   Hera (The Wife) 12
   Demeter (The Mother) 15
   Artemis (The Independent) 17
   Persephone (The Queen of the Underworld) 19
   Hestia (The Keeper of the Hearth) 21
   Athena (The Strategist and Wisdom) 23
   Hecate (The Witch and Guide of the Shadow) 26
   Ariadne (The Guide) 28
   Summary of Feminine Energies 32
   Workbook Unveil Your Inner Goddess 33

Chapter 2. Exploring the Gods. The Divine Masculine Energies 38
   Zeus (The King) 39
   Apollo (The Intellectual) 42
   Hermes (The Messenger) 44
   Dionysus (The Liberator) 46

Ares (The Warrior) 49

Hephaestus (The Craftsman) 52

Poseidon (The Power of the Deep) 54

Hades (The Lord of the Underworld) 57

Summary of the Inner Masculine Forces 60

Workbook. Discover the God Who Lives in You 61

Chapter 3. Divine Alchemy. The Dance of Couple's Attractions 66

Reveal the Power of Divine Interactions 67

Compatibility and Dynamics with Male Archetypes: 68

Relational Dynamics from the Male Perspective 82

Workbook Balancing Energies Within the Couple 87

Chapter 4. Shadow Work. The Dark Side of Your Archetype 90

The Hidden Power of Projection 91

Projections in Romantic Relationships 92

The Mirror Effect in Relationships 93

Wounds and Shadows: The Root of Projections 94

How Emotional Wounds Develop 95

The Age of Emotional Wound Formation 97

Who Has Discussed Them? 100

The Five Wounds in Detail 100

Shadows and Pain: How Divine Energies Reveal Wounds 104

Workbook Exercise: Connecting Your Wound to Your Shadow ... 108

Chapter 5.   Evolution of the Inner Divine Through Life's Stages 112

Examples of Inner Transformation 114

Famous Relationships: An Exploration of Divine Dynamics 117

Workbook Explore Your Divine Dynamics in Couples 128

Chapter 6. Shadow Work in Relationships 133

    Conflict as an Opportunity for Growth 135
    "I" Statements During Conflict 139
    I" Statements in Shadow Work 149
    The Cycle of Reconciliation 150
    Shadow Dialogues: A Practical Exercise 151

Conclusion. Embracing Growth Through Archetypes and Shadow Work 152
    Bibliography 154

Introduction

Human nature is full of complex and fascinating aspects, and one of them is how we are guided by deep forces that shape our relationships, often without us realizing it. These hidden impulses influence our desires, behaviors, and romantic choices. Archetypes, understood as primordial energies and universal patterns within our psyche, represent these forces and offer a key to better understanding ourselves and the people we love.

According to Jungian psychology, archetypes are not just theoretical concepts, but living, dynamic energies that operate within us, influencing every aspect of our emotional and relational lives. Each individual carries a combination of masculine and feminine archetypes that manifest at different stages of life, adapting to the challenges and experiences we encounter.

For example, a woman may feel guided by the archetype of Demeter, the protective mother, while at other stages of her life, the independent energy of Artemis may emerge. Similarly, a man may embody the archetype of Apollo, the rational one, or Dionysus, the emotional liberator. These archetypes not only influence attraction between people but also shape how we handle conflicts and tensions in relationships.

A crucial aspect of working with archetypes is the integration of the shadow, a concept developed by Carl Jung. The shadow represents those hidden parts of ourselves, often denied or repressed, that tend to surface in our most intimate relationships. Every archetype has a shadow side: for instance, the nurturing mother archetype can become smothering or overprotective, while the passionate lover can become possessive. Working with the shadow allows us to transform these aspects into resources, fostering personal and relational growth.

In this book, we will explore both feminine and masculine archetypes, analyzing how they manifest in our lives and how they interact in romantic relationships. Through practical examples, stories, and reflections, we will discover how these energies influence every stage of our relationships – from initial attraction to building a deep bond, and the challenges every couple faces.

This will not just be a theoretical journey: we will include practical exercises and reflections to help you recognize your archetypes, understand your partner's, and work with the shadow to improve your relationships. Our goal is to help you create a more authentic, deep, and conscious connection with yourself and the person you love.

Gods and Goddesses: The Dynamics in Romantic Relationships

Archetypes, though rooted in ancient traditions, offer a modern and insightful lens through which we can understand the dynamics of romantic relationships. Carl Gustav Jung first described archetypes as universal psychic forces that shape our behaviors and choices.

Building on Jung's foundational work, many contemporary authors have explored how these archetypes manifest in our romantic lives. Jean Shinoda Bolen, in Goddesses in Everywoman and Gods in Everyman, provides a detailed analysis of how masculine and feminine archetypes interact within us, influencing our relational patterns.

In addition to Bolen, other authors such as Robert Moore and Clarissa Pinkola Estés have expanded our understanding of how these archetypal energies guide both men and women. Moore's work on masculine archetypes and Estés' exploration of the wild feminine demonstrate that every person carries a mix of both energies, which can shape the dynamics of attraction, tension, and growth in relationships.

In this book, we will explore how these archetypal forces, represented by the gods and goddesses of Greek mythology, continue to resonate in our modern relationships. By examining these myths, we can see how the struggles, passions, and desires of ancient times mirror the same emotional challenges we face today. These archetypes offer powerful insights into the magnetic pull between partners, the conflicts that arise, and the potential for transformation within a relationship.

Chapter 1.

Exploring the Goddesses. The Divine Feminine Energies

The Goddess Who Lives in You

Archetypes are primordial energies that represent fundamental aspects of our psyche. Each archetype embodies a set of qualities, values, and ways of being that deeply influence how we live, our relationships, and how we see ourselves. Feminine archetypes specifically reflect the various expressions of femininity: from the passionate lover to the nurturing mother, from the independent woman to the transformative figure.

In Jungian psychology, archetypes are collective "models" that manifest on an individual level. Every person has a primary archetype that is active at a given moment in their life, while other archetypes remain in the "shadow," ready to emerge when circumstances call for them. There is no single correct form of femininity; these archetypes emerge at different times, reflecting the complexity and fluidity of human nature.

Each woman possesses a unique combination of these archetypal energies that adapt and transform according to the experiences she goes through. For example, a woman might embody the protective energy of Demeter when caring for her family, only to later enter a phase of greater independence and autonomy, manifesting the energy of Artemis. The dominant archetype at any given time can be replaced or balanced by others that surface in response to life's needs and challenges.

Ancestral Energies and Relationships

Archetypes influence not only how we are but also how we relate to others. For example, the Aphrodite archetype brings a powerful erotic and passionate energy, driving us to seek love and beauty. This archetype can generate attraction and magnetism in relationships but may also lead to insecurities or a tendency to idealize the partner excessively.

On the other hand, the Hera archetype is tied to stability, commitment, and fidelity. This energy can strengthen a relationship but may also introduce jealousy or rigidity in expectations. Understanding how these archetypes operate in relationships helps to build more balanced and conscious bonds, offering greater insight into our own behaviors and those of our partners.

Aphrodite (The Lover)

Aphrodite, the goddess of love, beauty, and passion, embodies the archetype of **the lover**. This archetype is one of the most powerful and complex expressions of femininity. It represents not only romantic love but also a deep connection with life's **pleasures**, **creativity**, and **sensuality**.

Aphrodite's energy is magnetic, drawing others in with charm, grace, and an irresistible allure. Women who embody Aphrodite often possess a natural beauty, which may not necessarily be physical, but one that radiates from within, attracting people with their liveliness and openness to emotional and sensual experiences.

Aphrodite's influence extends beyond romantic relationships. She governs our ability to appreciate beauty in all its forms, whether it be through art, nature, or personal expression. Creativity is a key part of Aphrodite's energy, inspiring people to engage in artistic pursuits or to live with an enhanced sensitivity to beauty and pleasure. Women with a strong

Aphrodite archetype are often driven to explore their creative potential, seeking outlets that allow them to express their passion, whether in the arts, fashion, design, or other creative fields.

Shadow Side: However, the Aphrodite archetype also comes with its challenges. This energy can sometimes lead to an overemphasis on physical attraction or external validation. A woman strongly influenced by Aphrodite might seek constant admiration, and this can lead to insecurity if the external affirmation she craves is not fulfilled. In relationships, this archetype can foster intense, passionate connections, but it may also cause a tendency to idealize the partner, placing them on a pedestal, which can lead to disappointment when the idealized image doesn't match reality.

Moreover, Aphrodite's archetype, if not balanced, can push a woman to prioritize the pursuit of pleasure and love over stability or long-term commitment. While this archetype brings emotional and sensual depth, it can sometimes struggle with the mundane realities of everyday life, such as building consistent, grounded relationships or handling responsibilities that do not align with the pursuit of passion and beauty.

On a deeper level, Aphrodite's influence taps into the core of a woman's ability to connect with her own body and emotions. This archetype invites her to embrace her sensuality and erotic nature without shame, celebrating the power of sexual attraction and emotional intimacy as essential parts of her identity. The challenge, however, is in balancing this powerful energy with the need for deeper, sustained emotional bonds, rather than fleeting connections.

Real-life example: Anna, a fashion designer, is deeply connected to the Aphrodite archetype. Her work is a reflection of her passion for beauty and elegance. She finds herself most inspired when creating, as she pours her emotions into each piece, seeing it as a form of artistic expression. In her personal life, Anna thrives in relationships that are emotionally intense, where she feels a profound sense of attraction and connection.

However, she has faced challenges when it comes to long-term stability. Her need for constant novelty and admiration in love often causes her to move on quickly, searching for a new flame when the passion fades. While her energy draws many towards her, she has had to learn how to balance this powerful Aphrodite force with the more grounded aspects of love, like commitment and emotional steadiness.

Hera (The Wife)

Hera, the queen of the gods and goddess of marriage and fidelity, represents the archetype of the **wife**. This archetype is deeply connected to the concepts of **commitment, stability, and loyalty**. Hera embodies the desire to build stable, long-lasting relationships based on deep bonds and the idea of a permanent union. A woman who identifies with this archetype tends to seek the security and protection that a committed relationship can offer, placing the creation and maintenance of a solid family or partnership at the center of her life.

Hera's energy focuses on fidelity and mutual commitment. It is the force that drives us to desire an exclusive bond and work to keep a long-term relationship alive, through honoring promises and sharing common values. This archetype is motivated by the idea of belonging, being chosen and loved exclusively, and the will to create something stable with the partner.

Shadow Side: However, Hera also has a shadow side. Her strong identification with the role of wife can lead to tendencies toward **jealousy, possessiveness**, and **control**, especially if the balance in the relationship feels threatened. The Hera archetype may cause a woman to feel vulnerable when she perceives that her partner is not honoring their commitment or when she feels threatened by other people or situations that could endanger the stability of the relationship.

In such cases, Hera's energy can transform into a rigid and **obsessive attachment**, where the **fear of abandonment** or **betrayal** dominates.

Additionally, a woman who strongly identifies with Hera may sacrifice important parts of herself, such as her sense of independence or personal desires, just to maintain the stability of the relationship.

Therefore, balance is crucial: Hera provides powerful energy of dedication and relationship-building, but it must be accompanied by the ability to maintain autonomy and a healthy sense of self within the relationship.

Real-life example: Lucia, a successful professional, has always been deeply committed to building a stable family. After marrying her partner, she invested time and energy into keeping their relationship strong, organizing shared moments and creating a safe and harmonious environment for the couple.

However, when her husband began to show signs of distance, Lucia experienced a deep sense of insecurity, fearing that their union might be threatened.

This led to moments of intense jealousy and an attempt to control the dynamics of the relationship, a shadow side of the Hera archetype that she had to learn to balance to avoid suffocating the relationship with her insecurities.

Demeter (The Mother)

Demeter, the goddess of the harvest and fertility, represents the archetype of the **mother**. This archetype is deeply connected to nurturing, care, and protection. Demeter embodies the energy of unconditional love and selflessness, often prioritizing the well-being of others, especially family and children, over her own needs. A woman who identifies with this archetype tends to find deep fulfillment in **caring** for others and creating a **safe, supportive environment** for those she loves.

The Demeter archetype manifests in the **drive to nurture** and **protect**, to provide sustenance not just in a physical sense but emotionally and spiritually as well. Women with a strong Demeter energy often feel called to serve, whether as mothers, caregivers, or in roles where they can support the growth and development of others. This archetype is associated with a deep sense of responsibility and the capacity to offer warmth and security, ensuring that those under her care feel loved and supported.

Shadow Side: However, like all archetypes, Demeter has a shadow side. A woman who over-identifies with Demeter may lose sight of her own needs, becoming overly **self-sacrificing**. She might fall into the trap of overprotectiveness, smothering those she cares for in an attempt to shield them from harm or difficulties. This can lead to feelings of **resentment** if her care is not reciprocated or appreciated, as she may struggle to set boundaries and prioritize her own well-being. In extreme cases, the Demeter archetype may manifest as **martyrdom**, where a woman sacrifices her own happiness and identity for the sake of others.

Demeter's story in Greek mythology reflects both the nurturing aspect and the challenges of this archetype. As the mother of Persephone, she experiences intense grief when her daughter is taken to the underworld by Hades. Demeter's devotion to Persephone drives her to search tirelessly for her, bringing fertility and growth to a halt as she grieves. This myth illustrates the power of the maternal bond but also the pain and loss that can come from over-identifying with the role of mother.

Real-life example: Maria, a social worker, embodies the Demeter archetype in her professional and personal life. She dedicates herself to helping vulnerable communities and finds great satisfaction in supporting others through difficult times. At home, she is a devoted mother, always putting the needs of her children first. However, over the years, Maria has struggled to maintain a balance between her role as caregiver and her personal desires. She often feels drained, having given so much to others without allowing herself the time or space to pursue her own interests. Maria has had to learn to set boundaries and recognize that her self-care is just as important as the care she offers to others.

Artemis (The Independent)

Artemis, the goddess of the hunt and the wilderness, represents the archetype of the **independent woman**. This archetype is deeply connected to **autonomy**, **personal freedom**, and a **strong sense of self**. Artemis embodies inner strength, the desire to explore the world on her own, and the ability to pursue her goals without relying on others. A woman who identifies with the Artemis archetype has a strong sense of independence and tends to seek fulfillment through self-sufficiency, exploration, and finding her own space, both physically and emotionally.

Artemis' energy centers on personal freedom and self-determination. Women who embody this archetype tend to prioritize their autonomy and fiercely protect their boundaries. Often, these women have a deep connection with nature or find solace in solitary activities that allow them to reflect and recharge. Artemis also represents sisterhood, the bond among women who support each other's individual growth without needing romantic ties or dependence on male figures.

Shadow Side: However, the Artemis archetype also has a shadow side. A woman strongly identified with this archetype may avoid emotional involvement or fear dependence on others, preferring to keep relationships distant to avoid losing her freedom. This can lead to **isolation** or difficulty in cultivating deep, meaningful relationships. Excessive self-sufficiency can turn into **a lack of vulnerability**, where emotional connections with others are seen as a threat.

Nevertheless, the Artemis archetype provides an example of courage and connection with one's inner truth. It is the archetype that encourages us to rediscover our strength, pursue personal goals with determination, and honor our path without seeking external validation. Artemis teaches that true independence does not mean being alone, but rather knowing who we are and what we want, remaining true to ourselves.

Real-life example: Giulia, a wildlife photographer, feels she embodies the energy of Artemis in her life. She loves spending long periods exploring wild landscapes, documenting the beauty of nature. She finds inspiration in solitude and in direct contact with the natural environment. Her relationships, even those with family and friends, often take second place to her desire to explore and maintain her independence. However, over time, Giulia has begun to realize that while she is satisfied with her autonomous lifestyle, she misses the deeper emotional connection with others and is learning to balance her desire for freedom with the ability to build meaningful relationships.

Persephone (The Queen of the Underworld)

Persephone, the goddess of the underworld and daughter of Demeter, represents the archetype of **transformation** and **emotional rebirth**. This archetype is deeply connected to the cycle of life, death, and renewal, symbolizing the journey into the depths of the unconscious and the discovery of personal power through transformation. A woman who identifies with Persephone often goes through significant periods of inner change, navigating the darker aspects of her psyche to emerge stronger and more self-aware.

The Persephone archetype embodies the duality of innocence and experience, **light** and **darkness**. In her myth, Persephone begins as the maiden, a symbol of purity and naiveté, but her abduction by Hades into the underworld forces her into a transformative journey. Through this descent, she gains wisdom and maturity, learning to embrace both the shadow aspects of her personality and her own inner power. As queen of the underworld, Persephone represents the ability to navigate the realms of the unconscious, confront fears, and find rebirth through emotional and psychological growth.

Women who resonate with the Persephone archetype often experience intense emotional shifts or life transitions. This archetype is associated with the willingness to embrace change, whether through personal loss, challenges, or difficult emotional experiences. Persephone invites women to explore their inner world, confront their hidden fears and insecurities, and find strength in their vulnerability. She teaches that true empowerment comes from integrating both the light and dark sides of the self.

Shadow Side: However, the shadow side of the Persephone archetype can manifest as **passivity** or a **sense of victimhood**. A woman strongly identified with Persephone may feel trapped in her circumstances, struggling to assert herself or make decisions. She might fall into patterns of waiting for change to happen rather than taking control of her own life. The challenge for Persephone is to recognize her own power and take an active role in shaping her destiny, rather than allowing external forces to define her.

In relationships, the Persephone archetype can lead to deep emotional connections, often with partners who bring out intense feelings of transformation or growth. These relationships may involve navigating emotional complexities or shadow work, where both partners are challenged to confront their hidden fears and desires. Persephone's journey teaches the value of emotional depth and the importance of embracing all aspects of one's self, even the darker or more difficult parts.

Real-life example: Sofia, a therapist, resonates strongly with the Persephone archetype. Having gone through a difficult divorce, she experienced a period of intense personal transformation, where she had to confront her deepest fears and insecurities.

This emotional descent into her own "underworld" helped Sofia to emerge stronger and more self-aware. In her work, she now helps others navigate their emotional struggles, guiding them through their own journeys of self-discovery and rebirth. However, Sofia has also had to learn how to balance her tendency to dwell in the depths of emotion with the need to stay grounded and present in her everyday life.

Hestia (The Keeper of the Hearth)

Hestia, the goddess of the hearth and home, represents the archetype of the **keeper of the hearth**, the **domestic center**, and **inner serenity**. This archetype is intimately connected to the care of both physical and spiritual spaces, emphasizing a connection with inner stillness and the creation of a safe, harmonious, and peaceful environment. Hestia embodies the centrality of warmth, stability, and the sacredness of everyday life, carrying with her an inner peace that reflects in family and personal life.

The Hestia archetype differs from other goddesses because she is not involved in conflicts, passions, or competitions. Her strength lies in her calmness and commitment to keeping the hearth's fire burning, a symbol of stability and continuity. A woman who embodies Hestia often focuses on herself in a contemplative way, striving to maintain balance and peace in her personal life and home. She is not swayed by turbulent emotions but finds comfort in routine, simplicity, and quiet.

Hestia also represents inner spirituality and introspection. In a woman's life, this archetype can manifest as the desire to find a sacred space and cultivate a sense of connection with herself and her spirituality. Women who embody this archetype tend to seek tranquility and avoid chaos, choosing to focus on inner well-being and maintaining a safe and serene space, both mentally and in their domestic life.

Shadow Side: The shadow side of Hestia appears when a woman withdraws too much into her inner world, isolating herself from others and the external world. Self-protection can turn into **excessive detachment from relationships** or a refusal to embrace change, preferring to **maintain the status**

quo out of fear of destabilizing her peace. In this state, a woman may become passive and disinterested in emotional growth or social connections.

Additionally, the Hestia archetype can lead to **excessive introversion**, where the need to maintain inner peace becomes an obstacle to interacting and sharing with others. This risk is particularly evident when the woman prefers to stay safe in her "inner hearth," avoiding any conflict or external challenges.

Real-life example: Marta, a holistic therapist, embodies the Hestia archetype in her daily life. She loves creating warm, harmonious spaces, both in her home and in the studio where she works with clients. Marta finds peace in meditation and spiritual practices that allow her to maintain a connection with her inner stillness. However, she has had to learn how to balance her desire for introspection with the need to open up more to interpersonal relationships, as she tends to withdraw too easily into her inner world when situations become too chaotic or emotionally intense.

Athena (The Strategist and Wisdom)

Athena, the goddess of wisdom, strategy, and war, represents the archetype of the **strategist and intellectual**

power. This archetype is strongly associated with **rational thinking, problem-solving,** and a **clear, logical approach to life**. Athena embodies the pursuit of knowledge and success, combining intellect with practical skills to achieve her goals. A woman who identifies with the Athena archetype tends to be driven, focused on her career or intellectual pursuits, and often values independence and self-sufficiency.

Athena is the embodiment of wisdom and clarity of thought. She excels in strategy, whether in personal decision-making, career, or leadership roles. Athena archetypes are typically organized, rational, and solution-oriented, seeking to navigate life with precision and efficiency. They are often drawn to roles that require clear thinking, discipline, and the ability to make strategic decisions, such as management, law, academia, or entrepreneurship. Athena is also the goddess of just warfare, symbolizing the ability to fight for what is right while maintaining moral integrity.

This archetype also represents a form of **independent thinking**. Women who embody Athena often avoid emotional entanglements that could cloud their judgment, choosing instead to focus on their goals. They prefer situations where they can use their intellect and strategic mindset to solve problems. Athena's wisdom is practical, grounded in real-world solutions rather than abstract ideals.

Shadow Side: Athena's shadow side emerges when a woman becomes **overly rational** or **disconnected from her**

emotions. A strong identification with this archetype can lead to emotional detachment or an excessive reliance on logic, often at the expense of deeper emotional connections. Athena may struggle with vulnerability, preferring to maintain control and avoid situations where emotions are involved. This can result in a disconnection from her own emotional world or the emotional needs of those around her, which may create difficulties in personal relationships.

Additionally, women who identify too strongly with Athena may become overly **competitive** or career-focused, sometimes at the cost of their personal lives. They may have difficulty balancing work and relationships, or may prioritize success and achievement to the detriment of their well-being.

Real-life example: Laura, a successful attorney, embodies the Athena archetype in both her professional and personal life. She thrives in her career, where her strategic thinking and sharp intellect help her navigate complex legal cases. Laura is known for her clarity of thought and her ability to remain calm under pressure. However, she has struggled to connect emotionally with those closest to her, often prioritizing her career and intellectual pursuits over her personal relationships. Over time, Laura has realized the importance of balancing her rational mind with her emotional world, working to integrate her logical strengths with more vulnerability and emotional awareness.

Hecate (The Witch and Guide of the Shadow)

Hecate, the goddess of magic, crossroads, and hidden mysteries, represents the archetype of **the witch** and the guide through moments of transition and transformation. This archetype is deeply connected to the power of intuition, the world of the unconscious, and the ability to navigate through the darker phases of life. Hecate is the guardian of the shadow and invisible forces, symbolizing the wisdom to confront the unknown and guide oneself or others through inner challenges.

Hecate embodies the **inner strength** needed to explore what is hidden or feared, inviting women to face their deepest fears and embrace the transformation that comes from it. She is associated with moments of crisis and change, when a person is forced to reckon with their shadow and aspects of their psyche that are usually ignored or repressed. Women who embody Hecate tend to be aware of life's complexities and are able to find light even in times of darkness.

Hecate is also a spiritual guide. Women strongly connected to this archetype are often drawn to the occult, magic, or deep spiritual practices. This archetype encourages a connection with one's intuition and inner worlds, bringing awareness and wisdom not just through rationality but also through feeling and intuition. Hecate also represents the courage to stand at the crossroads of life—those difficult decisions or critical phases where change is inevitable—knowing that, from these transitions, one can emerge wiser and stronger.

Shadow Side: Hecate's shadow side emerges when a woman becomes **too attracted to the darker side of life** or **isolates herself** excessively in her inner world. She might fall into the trap of constantly exploring the shadowy aspects of existence, losing touch with reality and with everyday relationships. An excessive identification with Hecate can also lead to a solitary life, where a person prefers to be alone rather than connect with others, especially if she fears vulnerability or sharing her darker sides.

Moreover, Hecate can represent a form of **resistance to change**. Despite being the goddess of crossroads, a woman too attached to this archetype might become stuck in fear of transitions, unable to make decisions or move forward. She might retreat into a world of mystery, avoiding the challenges and responsibilities of practical life.

Real-life example: Silvia, a tarot reader and practitioner of magic, embodies the Hecate archetype. For years, she has provided guidance to those at life's crossroads, helping people make decisions through tarot readings and rituals. Silvia has always felt a strong connection to the invisible world and magic, seeing herself as a guide for those facing the unknown. However, recently she found herself in a phase of significant personal transformation: a painful separation and the closure of her shop have forced her to reassess her path. For the first time, Silvia must use her knowledge of shadow work and transformation for herself, confronting deep fears and finding a new direction in life. This process is teaching her that, even in the darkest moments, there is always a way toward rebirth.

Ariadne (The Guide)

Although Ariadne is not a goddess like the other figures in this chapter, she plays a significant role in Greek mythology and represents a powerful archetype of **guidance, support, and navigating through complexity**. Ariadne is most famously known for helping Theseus escape the labyrinth by giving him a ball of thread, allowing him to find his way back after defeating the Minotaur. This act of guidance and problem-solving makes her an essential archetypal figure, even though she is often overshadowed by the more prominent goddesses of Greek mythology.

In psychological and mythological studies, particularly in the work of **James Hillman**, a key figure in the development of archetypal psychology, Ariadne is seen as an archetype of **the guide and mediator**. Hillman often explores how figures like Ariadne symbolize our ability to navigate through emotional or psychological labyrinths, helping us find solutions in seemingly impossible situations. Her story offers a metaphor for how we can use our inner wisdom, or external support, to untangle complex problems and emerge with clarity and direction.

Ariadne embodies the power of **practical wisdom**—the ability to see through complicated circumstances and offer solutions that may not be obvious at first glance. She is the archetype of someone who helps others find their way, especially when life presents complex challenges or emotional turmoil. Women who resonate with the Ariadne archetype often serve as guides or problem solvers for others, using their insight and intuition to help people navigate through difficult situations.

Ariadne also represents the theme of **transformation through abandonment**. After helping Theseus, she was famously abandoned by him on the island of Naxos, where she was later found and married by Dionysus. This part of her story reflects the themes of loss and recovery, symbolizing how we can find renewal and a new path even after experiencing betrayal or disappointment.

Shadow Side: The shadow side of the Ariadne archetype may emerge when a woman **becomes too focused on guiding or solving others' problems**, losing sight of her own needs and desires. Ariadne, as a guide, can sometimes fall into the trap of **sacrificing her own well-being** for the sake of others. Additionally, there is the risk of becoming entangled in dysfunctional situations, similar to her involvement with Theseus, where she may help someone who ultimately abandons or mistreats her.

Ariadne's story also serves as a warning about the potential to give too much without receiving reciprocal support, which can lead to feelings of abandonment or neglect. Women strongly identified with this archetype may need to be careful about balancing their desire to help others with ensuring they are also cared for and appreciated in return.

Real-life example: Claudia, a project manager at a large firm, embodies the Ariadne archetype in her ability to guide her team through complex projects. She often acts as the mediator and problem solver, helping her colleagues untangle complicated issues and navigate through tight deadlines. Claudia has a talent for finding practical solutions, but sometimes she feels drained by always being the one others turn to for guidance. Recently, after a personal setback in her romantic life, Claudia realized that she had been investing so much energy in helping others that she had neglected her own emotional needs. Now, she is learning to balance her role as a guide with taking time for herself and ensuring her own path is clear.

Summary of Feminine Energies

Archetype	Main Characteristics	Shadow Side
Aphrodite (The Lover)	Passion, love, beauty, emotional creativity. Deep connection with sensuality and the expression of love.	Seeking external validation, idealizing the partner, superficial relationships.
Hera (The Wife)	Stability, commitment, loyalty. Desire to build long-lasting relationships based on faithfulness.	Jealousy, possessiveness, excessive attachment to the partner.
Demeter (The Mother)	Nurturing, protection, unconditional care. Driven by the need to support and provide security for others.	Overprotection, excessive self-sacrifice, neglecting personal needs.
Artemis (The Independent)	Autonomy, freedom, self-connection. Strong sense of independence and self-determination.	Emotional detachment, avoiding intimacy, isolation.
Persephone (The Queen of the Underworld)	Transformation, emotional rebirth, connection with the unconscious. Wisdom derived from deep experiences.	Passivity, sense of victimhood, difficulty in making decisions and moving forward.
Hestia (The Keeper of the Hearth)	Inner peace, care for the home, spiritual harmony. Connection with inner tranquility and spirituality.	Emotional isolation, excessive withdrawal into one's inner world.
Athena (The Strategist and Wisdom)	Wisdom, strategic thinking, rationality. Skill in solving problems with logic and discipline.	Emotional detachment, excessive rationality, difficulties in personal relationships.
Hecate (The Witch and Guide of the Shadow)	Intuition, guide during transitions, connection with the shadow. Ability to navigate the dark side of the psyche.	Isolation, attraction to the dark side of life, resistance to change.
Ariadne (The Guide)	Practical wisdom, guiding through complex situations. Ability to find solutions and help others in difficult moments.	Self-sacrifice for others, risk of abandonment or betrayal in relationships.

Workbook
Unveil Your Inner Goddess

Answer the following questions by choosing the option that best describes you. At the end of the test, tally your responses to see which archetype (goddess) dominates your life right now.

1. When facing a challenge, how do you usually respond?

a) I focus on maintaining harmony and supporting those around me.
b) I try to solve the problem rationally and strategically.
c) I trust my intuition and explore deeper, hidden aspects of the situation.
d) I rely on my independence and face the challenge on my own.
e) I try to maintain the stability and security of the relationship or situation.
f) I try to understand how the challenge can transform me emotionally.

2. How do people who know you best usually describe you?

a) Nurturing and protective.
b) Rational and wise.
c) Mysterious and intuitive.
d) Independent and strong.
e) Loyal and committed.
f) Passionate and captivating.

3. Which of these situations makes you most uncomfortable?

a) When someone doesn't appreciate my efforts to care and protect.
b) When I can't plan or strategize effectively.
c) When I'm forced to ignore my intuitive or spiritual side.
d) When my freedom is limited or compromised.
e) When I perceive a threat to the stability or loyalty of a relationship.
f) When the attraction or passion in my life fades.

4. What gives you the most energy?

a) Taking care of the people I love.
b) Solving complex problems with logic and strategy.
c) Exploring mysteries and understanding hidden aspects of a situation.

d) Feeling autonomous and free.
e) Creating stable and lasting relationships.
f) Feeling a deep emotional connection and passion in my relationships.

5. What is your main goal in life?

a) Taking care of my family or loved ones.
b) Achieving personal and professional success through wisdom and critical thinking.
c) Discovering and understanding the hidden truths of the world and myself.
d) Being independent and living by my own rules.
e) Building stable and trustworthy relationships.
f) Exploring love, beauty, and emotional creativity.

6. When do you feel most useful to others?

a) When I support them emotionally or physically.
b) When I help them solve complex problems with logic.
c) When I provide them with spiritual insights or advice.
d) When I encourage them to be independent.
e) When I offer stability and loyalty in relationships.
f) When I guide them to find solutions during difficult times.

7. What makes you most satisfied in daily life?

a) Taking care of the people I love.
b) Planning and achieving my goals.
c) Connecting spiritually or reflecting inwardly.
d) Finding my balance and inner peace.
e) Building a stable and loyal relationship.
f) Finding beauty and passion in my daily experiences.

Results Interpretation

Now tally how many times you selected each letter and discover which goddess/archetype dominates your life:

Mostly A: Demeter (The Mother) – Your dominant archetype is linked to the energy of care, nurturing, and protection.

Mostly B: Athena (The Strategist and Wisdom) – You are guided by rationality and strategic thinking. You enjoy solving problems with logic and discipline.

Mostly C: Hecate (The Witch and Guide of the Shadow) – Your dominant archetype is connected to intuition, spirituality, and exploring hidden mysteries.

Mostly D: Artemis (The Independent) – Your life is guided by autonomy and independence. You prefer to act according to your own rules.

Mostly E: Hera (The Wife) – You are focused on commitment, loyalty, and building stable and lasting relationships.

Mostly F: Aphrodite (The Lover) – You are guided by passion, love, and beauty. Emotional and romantic relationships are central to your life.

If you often selected F in question 6: Ariadne (The Guide) – Your dominant archetype is related to practical wisdom and the ability to guide others through difficult times, much like Ariadne with the thread of the labyrinth.

Chapter 2.

Exploring the Gods.
The Divine Masculine Energies

The masculine archetypes represent profound forces that influence men's behavior, ambitions, and relationships. Each archetype embodies a specific mode of expressing masculine energy, ranging from control and power to creativity, communication, and passion. Just like the feminine archetypes, these masculine ones are present in the psyche of every individual and can manifest at different points in life, depending on the circumstances and challenges a man faces.

In Jungian psychology, masculine archetypes are universal models that represent typical modes of leadership, rationality, strength, and intuition. However, as with the feminine archetypes, there is no rigid or exclusive form of masculinity: each man is a dynamic combination of archetypal energies that can emerge in different ways during various life phases or relationships. Some men may feel closer to the rational energy of Apollo, while others may resonate more with the passionate force of Ares or the emotional spontaneity of Dionysus.

These archetypes not only act on the individual level but also significantly influence romantic, professional, and social relationships. Understanding which masculine archetypes dominate a man's life, or that of his partner, can offer insights into interpreting complex relationship dynamics, deep attractions, or interpersonal conflicts.

In this chapter, we will explore the main masculine archetypes through the lens of relationship dynamics, examining how each archetype influences how a man relates to power, intellect, communication, emotion, and strength. These archetypes not only shape a man's behavior but also often determine the types of relationships he builds and how he interacts with his partner.

Let's delve into each masculine archetype in detail, connecting them to the typical dynamics that emerge in relationships and daily interactions.

Zeus (The King)

Zeus, the king of the gods on Olympus, is the archetype that embodies **power**, **authority**, and the will to govern. As the lord of the sky and earth, Zeus is the one who makes supreme decisions, sets rules, and issues orders. Men who embody this archetype are often driven by the need to lead and control their own lives and those of others. They are natural leaders, ambitious and assertive, with a great capacity to influence the world around them. Zeus is the driving force behind the desire to achieve great goals and reach positions of power and responsibility.

The Zeus archetype manifests through a strong will to power and decisive leadership. A man guided by this archetype does not shy away from making difficult decisions, is a visionary, and has a clear understanding of what he wants to achieve. However, his desire for control can lead him to be authoritarian or manipulative, especially when he feels his power is threatened. Zeus is not only a leader in the political or social sense but also a protector of institutions and traditional structures. In personal relationships, this archetype appears as a partner who seeks to establish a secure and stable environment for his loved ones but tends to impose his will and direct the course of the relationship.

In a relationship, a man with the Zeus archetype tends to want to be the **dominant figure**, the one who makes the most important decisions and guides the direction of the couple or family. He wants to be seen as the **pillar of the relationship**, the one who protects and provides **stability**. Zeus is often attracted to partners who appreciate or respect his power and leadership. However, his tendency toward control can lead to imbalanced dynamics if he cannot recognize the needs and opinions of the other person. In some cases, a man with a strong Zeus archetype may become possessive or tyrannical, expecting obedience and loyalty without compromise.

The challenge for Zeus is learning to balance his desire for control with the ability to listen and respect his partner's point of view, avoiding stifling their freedom.

Zeus's Shadow Side: The shadow side of the Zeus archetype emerges when the need for power becomes excessive, leading to **authoritarian, manipulative,** or **oppressive behavior**. A man strongly identified with this archetype may become overly rigid or domineering, unable to tolerate criticism or compromise. In times of stress or insecurity, Zeus may react by tightening his control over those around him, trying to maintain power at all costs. This tendency can create **toxic relational dynamics**, where the partner feels crushed or subordinate. In his shadow side, Zeus may **lose sight of empathy** and **listening,** focusing solely on his will to power.

Real-life example: Marco, a successful entrepreneur, embodies the Zeus archetype in his career and relationships. He has built a prosperous business and is known for his ability to make quick and decisive decisions. In his marriage, he sees himself as the primary protector of the family and often assumes the role of leader. However, his tendency to always want control has caused tensions with his wife, who desires more balance in family decisions. Over time, Marco has learned to balance his desire for leadership with the need to listen and respect others' viewpoints, striving not to let his power become an obstacle in his personal relationships.

Apollo (The Intellectual)

Apollo, the god of the sun, light, and knowledge, represents the archetype of the **intellectual** and **rational mind**. As a deity associated with music, poetry, and medicine, Apollo symbolizes clarity, order, and the pursuit of knowledge.

Men who embody this archetype value logic, reason, and intellectual achievements. They are often driven by a desire to understand the world through analysis and structure, seeking to bring light and wisdom into situations of confusion.

The Apollo archetype is linked to the power of reason and mental clarity. Men connected to this archetype are methodical and deliberate, preferring to tackle life's challenges with a structured plan. They excel in fields that require logic, intellect, and a disciplined approach, such as science, law, or academia. However, their rationality can also become a weakness if they distance themselves too much from emotions or underestimate the importance of empathy.

In relationships, an Apollo man tends to value communication, intellectual compatibility, and shared goals. He seeks a partner who appreciates deep discussions and decision-making based on logic. While they can offer stability and clarity, their focus on rationality may create emotional distance with their partner, making them seem distant or cold. The challenge for Apollo is to balance his intellect with a deeper emotional connection.

Apollo's Shadow Side: Apollo's shadow side emerges when his focus on logic becomes excessive, leading to **emotional detachment** and **coldness**. A man overly identified with this archetype may prioritize reason to the point of ignoring feelings, both his own and others', creating distance in relationships. Additionally, his desire for control and perfection can turn into **rigidity**, limiting his ability to adapt to situations that require intuition or empathy.

Real-life example: David, a software engineer, embodies the Apollo archetype in his ability to solve complex problems and plan with precision. However, in his relationship, he has had to learn to connect emotionally with his partner, overcoming his natural tendency to avoid emotional conversations.

Hermes (The Messenger)

Hermes, the messenger of the gods, represents the archetype of **communication**, **adaptability**, and **movement**. As a god of trade, travelers, and boundaries, Hermes embodies the ability to connect, communicate, and navigate through different worlds. Men who resonate with this archetype are often flexible, charismatic, and quick-thinking. They are skilled at bridging gaps between people, ideas, and perspectives, often serving as mediators or facilitators in various situations.

Hermes is also known for his cunning and cleverness. He can adapt to new environments with ease and find creative solutions to complex problems. This archetype is deeply associated with the art of persuasion, the gift of storytelling, and the ability to navigate complex social dynamics.

Men connected to Hermes are often curious, always looking for new experiences and opportunities. They thrive in environments that allow for creativity and change, such as media, technology, or entrepreneurship. Hermes men are excellent communicators and can quickly adjust their approach to suit different situations. Their charm and wit make them natural negotiators and problem-solvers.

However, the same flexibility that allows them to navigate different spaces can also make them restless or indecisive..

In relationships, a man with a strong Hermes archetype is often engaging and fun to be around. He values open communication and is likely to be a great conversationalist. Hermes men are typically **spontaneous** and bring a sense of **adventure** to their relationships. They seek partners who appreciate their fluid nature and are open to change.

However, their adaptability and desire for freedom can sometimes make it difficult for them to commit fully to a relationship. They may avoid deeper emotional connections or long-term stability, preferring instead to keep things light and flexible. The challenge for Hermes is to balance his love of freedom with the need for emotional depth and commitment in relationships.

Hermes's Shadow Side: The shadow side of Hermes emerges when his flexibility turns into **inconsistency** or **deceit**. A man overly identified with this archetype may become **unreliable** or **manipulative**, using his communication skills to deceive others or avoid responsibility. In his shadow, Hermes can be seen as the trickster, using charm and wit to get what he wants without regard for the consequences. This behavior can lead to superficial relationships and a lack of trust from others.

Additionally, Hermes's constant search for new experiences may lead to a sense of restlessness or dissatisfaction, where he is always looking for the next opportunity rather than appreciating the present moment.

Real-life example: Tom, a successful entrepreneur in the tech industry, embodies the Hermes archetype. He is known for his ability to network and build relationships quickly, as well as his knack for finding creative solutions to business challenges. However, Tom sometimes struggles with staying focused on one project for too long, as he is constantly drawn to new opportunities and ideas. In his personal life, this restlessness has made it difficult for him to commit fully to long-term relationships, as he prefers to keep things spontaneous and flexible.

Dionysus (The Liberator)

Dionysus, the god of wine, celebration, and ecstasy, embodies the archetype of **emotional freedom, spontaneity, and sensual pleasure**. As the god of chaos and liberation, Dionysus represents everything that breaks away from norms, rules, and societal conventions. Men resonating with this archetype tend to live life with passion, seeking pleasure and sensory experience in everything they do. Dionysus carries the energy of celebration, joy, and deep connection with emotions and the body.

While other male archetypes may prioritize control or rationality, Dionysus is the force that pushes men to let go, **embrace chaos**, and follow their desires. His energy is not contained or limited but rather fluid, capable of transforming those who embrace it. This archetype is also closely linked to creativity, artistic expression, and the pursuit of inner truth through deep and emotional experiences.

Men with this archetype are often spontaneous, unafraid to show their emotions, and guided by momentary desires. They are drawn to intense experiences, whether in art, music, sex, or celebration, and seek to live life to the fullest. Creativity plays a central role in their lives, and many Dionysus men express themselves through artistic forms or experiences that connect them to deep, spiritual emotions.

However, this same passion for freedom and ecstasy can also lead to **self-destruction** if not balanced. Dionysus, with his desire for indulgence and pleasure, can become excessive, leading to addictions or irresponsible behaviors.

In relationships, a Dionysus man is an engaging, sensual, and passionate partner. He approaches relationships with **emotional and physical intensity**, seeking **deep and authentic connections**. Dionysus values authenticity and desires relationships where he can be himself without filters. His ability to connect with emotions and pleasure often makes these relationships very passionate and free from societal conventions.

However, the challenge for a Dionysus man lies in finding the balance between his need for freedom and commitment to his partner. He may struggle to maintain a stable or long-term relationship, as his desire to explore new experiences may conflict with the need for stability and responsibility. In some cases, the Dionysus archetype can lead to a constant search for pleasure and avoidance of committed relationships or everyday responsibilities.

Dionysus' Shadow Side: The shadow side of Dionysus emerges when his desire for freedom and pleasure becomes excessive, leading to self-destructive or irresponsible behavior. A man too identified with this archetype may fall into addictions or live a chaotic life, unable to take responsibility or maintain stable relationships. The need to escape reality can lead him to avoid the challenges of daily life, constantly seeking pleasure without regard for consequences. Dionysus in his shadow can also experience intense emotional swings, oscillating between euphoria and despair.

Real-life example: Luca, a music artist, embodies the Dionysus archetype. Known for his charismatic performances and his ability to connect emotionally with the audience, Luca lives each creative and sensory experience intensely. However, his desire for freedom sometimes leads him to neglect responsibilities, which compromises his personal relationships.

Ares (The Warrior)

Ares, the god of war, embodies the archetype of the warrior, representing **physical strength, courage, and raw passion**. As a fierce and aggressive deity, Ares symbolizes the untamed and primal energy within men, the drive to fight for what they believe in, and the willingness to confront challenges head-on. Men who resonate with this archetype often have a strong **sense of purpose** and are motivated by their **desire to conquer obstacles** and defend their values.

While other masculine archetypes may seek to lead, strategize, or communicate, Ares channels his energy into action. His approach is direct, intense, and often driven by instinct. He is not concerned with diplomacy or intellectual analysis—he is the force that acts swiftly and decisively. This archetype also encompasses the passion and intensity found in personal and romantic relationships, where Ares men tend to express their emotions boldly and without hesitation.

Ares embodies a fierce competitive spirit. Men connected to this archetype are typically **assertive**, and **ready to take**

risks. They thrive in situations that require boldness and physical endurance, such as sports, military service, or any field that demands quick and decisive action. Ares men are often protective of those they care about and will not hesitate to confront any threat to their loved ones or values. This archetype also connects to a deep sense of justice and the drive to stand up for what is right, regardless of the challenges faced.

However, the intensity of Ares can sometimes be overwhelming. His need for action and confrontation may lead to **impulsiveness** or **aggression**, making it difficult for him to find balance or maintain long-term relationships without conflict.

In romantic relationships, an Ares man is passionate, direct, and deeply committed. He values intensity and physical connection, and his love can be as fierce as his approach to conflict. An Ares man seeks partners who can match his passion and who appreciate his protective nature. However, his impulsive behavior can sometimes lead to disagreements or power struggles, as he tends to act without considering the consequences. The challenge for Ares is to learn patience and emotional awareness, understanding that not every situation requires immediate action or conflict.

Ares's Shadow Side: The shadow side of Ares emerges when his aggression and impulsiveness go unchecked. A man overly identified with Ares may become prone to **anger,**

conflict, and even **violence.** His tendency to act without thinking can lead to reckless decisions, alienating those around him. In his shadow, Ares may also become overly competitive, viewing every interaction as a battle to be won, which can harm relationships and personal growth.

Additionally, Ares's shadow can manifest as a **lack of empathy**, where his focus on action and victory blinds him to the emotional needs of others. To grow, Ares must learn to channel his strength in constructive ways and develop greater emotional intelligence, recognizing that true power often comes from understanding and collaboration, not just physical dominance or conflict.

Real-life example: Roberto, a firefighter, embodies the Ares archetype in his dedication to action and his willingness to put himself at risk for the safety of others. His bravery and determination have earned him respect from his colleagues and community. However, in his personal life, Roberto sometimes struggles with his impulsive nature, often acting on instinct in relationships and finding it difficult to communicate calmly during disagreements. Over time, he has learned the importance of patience and understanding, recognizing that not every challenge requires immediate action.

Hephaestus (The Craftsman)

Hephaestus, the god of fire and metalworking, represents the archetype of the craftsman and embodies **creativity, technical skill,** and **perseverance**. As the divine smith, Hephaestus is responsible for forging the weapons and tools of the gods, symbolizing mastery over the material world through labor, innovation, and craftsmanship. Unlike other gods who may rule through power or intellect, Hephaestus gains his significance through his ability to create, shaping both physical objects and his destiny with his hands.

Hephaestus is often depicted as an outcast among the gods, having been cast from Mount Olympus due to his physical deformity or after an altercation between his parents, Zeus and Hera. Despite these setbacks, Hephaestus does not let rejection define him. Instead, he channels his energy into perfecting his craft, using the fire of his forge to create items of great beauty and strength. His story is one of resilience, determination, and overcoming adversity through skill and patience.

The Hephaestus archetype is characterized by a deep connection to work, craft, and creation. Men who resonate with this archetype are often dedicated to mastering their craft, whether it is in the arts, engineering, or any profession requiring skill and precision. They take pride in their work, finding fulfillment in the act of creating and problem-solving. Hephaestus men are patient and resilient, able to work through challenges methodically and with determination.

However, they may also struggle with feelings of **isolation** or **inadequacy**, especially if they perceive that their worth is only tied to their output. Like Hephaestus, they may feel marginalized or underappreciated for their contributions, despite their central role in building and sustaining the world around them.

In relationships, a man embodying the Hephaestus archetype is likely to be **loyal, dedicated,** and **supportive**. He is a provider who may express his love through acts of service, creating stability and security for his loved ones. However, his focus on work and craft can sometimes lead to emotional distance, as he may struggle to communicate his feelings or prioritize relationships over his projects. The challenge for Hephaestus is learning to balance his dedication to work with emotional intimacy, recognizing that his worth extends beyond what he produces.

Hephaestus's Shadow Side: The shadow side of the Hephaestus archetype emerges when the need for **productivity** and **perfection becomes obsessive**. A man overly identified with this archetype may become **consumed by his work**, neglecting other aspects of life such as relationships and personal well-being. He may also struggle with self-worth, believing that his value lies solely in his ability to produce or solve problems. In his shadow, Hephaestus may isolate himself, driven by a fear of rejection or a desire to prove his worth through his creations.

Real-life example: Stefano, a skilled blacksmith and artisan, embodies the Hephaestus archetype. Known for his intricate metalwork and ability to transform raw materials into beautiful, functional pieces, Stefano takes pride in the patience and precision required by his craft. However, he often struggles with feelings of isolation, spending long hours in his workshop and finding it difficult to connect emotionally with others. Over time, Stefano has learned to balance his passion for work with a deeper appreciation for personal relationships, recognizing that his value extends beyond his creations.

Poseidon (The Power of the Deep)

Poseidon, the god of the sea, represents the archetype of hidden **power** and **deep emotions**. As the lord of the oceans, Poseidon embodies control over nature's unpredictable forces and the emotional undercurrents within us. His energy is powerful and primal, reflecting emotional currents that can be calm on the surface but turbulent in their depths.

Men who resonate with this archetype often possess **intense emotional energy**, capable of sudden outbursts of anger or passion, much like an unexpected storm.

Poseidon doesn't just rule the physical waters; he also represents dominance over the emotional world and unconscious drives. While Zeus governs order, Poseidon symbolizes the chaotic potential that can arise from repressed emotions and unresolved inner conflicts. Those who identify with this archetype often find themselves led by their emotions, oscillating between calm and sudden emotional storms. These men are typically **protective, sometimes dominant** in their relationships, seeking to control both their own emotions and those of the people around them.

In relationships, a man embodying Poseidon's archetype is often passionate and possessive. He experiences love with intensity and depth, but may struggle to control his emotions, reacting strongly when feeling threatened or betrayed. This behavior can lead to conflicts with his partner, as Poseidon can be impulsive and sometimes irrational in his reactions. However, his deep emotional connection allows him to be a highly sensitive and protective partner. His desire to dominate situations can become a strength if he learns to manage his emotions without being overwhelmed by impulsivity.

Poseidon's Shadow Side: Poseidon's shadow side emerges when his emotional intensity becomes destructive. A man overly identified with this archetype can be irritable and unpredictable, reacting with excessive anger or jealousy. His emotions may become unmanageable, leading to **self-destructive behaviors** or **harm to his relationships**. In this state, Poseidon can become tyrannical, trying to control everything and everyone around him without considering the emotional consequences. To overcome his shadow side, Poseidon must learn to channel his emotions constructively and develop the ability to reflect before acting. Only through mastering his emotional energy can he achieve true stability and harmony in his relationships and life.

Real-Life Example: Marco, a criminal defense attorney, embodies the Poseidon archetype. His determination and intense emotional energy make him a tireless advocate for his clients, fighting with great passion. However, his impulsiveness often leads to conflicts with colleagues and tense moments in his personal relationships due to overreactions. Over time, Marco has learned to manage his emotions and channel his energy in more constructive ways, balancing his passion with the calm required to handle complex situations effectively.

Hades (The Lord of the Underworld)

Hades, the god of the underworld, represents the archetype of **death, transformation**, and the hidden realms of the psyche. As the ruler of the underworld, Hades governs the afterlife and the profound, mysterious forces of life and death. His archetype invites reflection on mortality, inner transformation, and the acceptance of the darker, often hidden, aspects of existence. Unlike other gods who engage with the living world, Hades presides over the realm of shadows, offering a path to deep introspection and personal growth through understanding life's ultimate mysteries.

Often misunderstood as a fearsome figure, Hades is not inherently malevolent. His archetype symbolizes the inevitability of change, the process of endings that lead to new beginnings, and the wisdom gained through exploring the deepest layers of the psyche. Hades governs the unknown aspects of our lives—mysteries, fears, and the ultimate questions of existence.

The Hades archetype is associated with introversion, depth, and transformation. Men connected with Hades are often **introspective**, drawn to the mysteries of life and death, and unafraid to explore the darker corners of their minds. This archetype thrives on the invisible and the unconscious, guiding individuals to confront their fears and accept the inevitability of death and loss as part of the natural cycle of life.

Men embodying the Hades archetype tend to value **solitude and deep reflection**. They are less interested in the superficial or material aspects of life, focusing instead on inner growth, wisdom, and personal transformation. Their energy is quiet but profound, and they often provide deep insights into aspects of life that others might avoid.

In relationships, a man embodying Hades may be deeply introspective and emotionally reserved. He values depth in his connections and seeks a partner who can engage with him on a deep emotional and intellectual level. However, his introversion may make him seem distant or difficult to reach, as he may struggle to express his emotions openly or need space and solitude frequently.

Hades men can be loyal and stable partners, but they require a relationship that allows them the freedom to explore their inner world without feeling pressured to conform to social expectations. The challenge for Hades is to balance his need for solitude with the emotional intimacy required in relationships, learning to share his inner world with others instead of retreating entirely into it.

Hades' Shadow Side: The shadow side of Hades emerges when his desire for solitude turns into isolation, or when introspection becomes overwhelming. A man overly identified with Hades may withdraw from life, becoming disconnected from the world around him and falling into states of melancholy or depression. His focus on the darker aspects of existence can lead him to become **pessimistic or fatalistic**, losing sight of the balance between life and death.

In his shadow form, Hades may also struggle with **feelings of alienation or abandonment**, believing that others cannot understand his inner depth or appreciate his emotional complexity. To overcome his shadow side, Hades must learn to integrate his deep understanding of the psyche with a sense of connection to the living world, finding a balance between introspection and external action.

Real-Life Example: Giovanni, a therapist specializing in trauma recovery, embodies the Hades archetype. He is deeply committed to helping his clients explore their inner worlds and process difficult emotions related to loss and grief. While Giovanni excels at guiding others through their emotional challenges, he often finds it difficult to open up about his own feelings, preferring solitude and introspection. Over time, he has learned to balance his inner work with the need to cultivate relationships and maintain a connection to the outside world.

Summary of the Inner Masculine Forces

Archetype	Main Characteristics	Shadow Side
Zeus (The King)	Leadership, authority, control. Seeks order and stability.	Authoritarianism, obsession with control, domination.
Apollo (The Intellectual)	Logic, clarity, rationality. Focuses on intellectual pursuits and structure.	Emotional detachment, coldness, lack of empathy.
Hermes (The Messenger)	Communication, adaptability, flexibility. Skilled at connecting people and ideas.	Inconsistency, deceit, manipulation, avoidance of commitment.
Dionysus (The Liberator)	Emotional freedom, spontaneity, passion, creativity. Seeks pleasure and self-expression.	Self-destructive behavior, hedonism, lack of responsibility.
Ares (The Warrior)	Strength, courage, action. Driven by purpose and ready to confront challenges.	Aggression, impulsiveness, conflict-seeking.
Hephaestus (The Craftsman)	Creativity, skill, resilience. Focuses on craft and problem-solving through persistence.	Isolation, workaholism, feelings of inadequacy, emotional distance.
Poseidon (The Power of the Deep)	Emotional intensity, passion, dominance. Seeks control over deep emotions and forces.	Emotional outbursts, possessiveness, impulsivity.
Hades (The Lord of the Underworld)	Mystery, introspection, transformation. Connected to mortality and inner exploration.	Isolation, depression, disconnection from life, emotional withdrawal.

Workbook.
Discover the God Who Lives in You

For each of the following questions, choose the option that resonates most with you. At the end, tally your choices to discover which archetype is dominant in your personality.

1. How do you typically handle leadership situations?

A) I take charge naturally and expect others to follow my lead.
B) I rely on logic and reason to guide people effectively.
C) I adapt quickly and find ways to communicate to unite people.
D) I encourage others to embrace their freedom and emotions.
E) I'm ready to confront any challenge head-on, no hesitation.
F) I prefer to focus on building things and solving problems.
G) I tend to rely on my emotional instincts to manage complex situations.
H) I reflect deeply on the situation before acting, valuing quiet wisdom.

2. How do you approach relationships?

A) I seek stability and prefer to lead the relationship with confidence.
B) I value intellectual connection and mutual understanding.
C) I enjoy keeping things light and flexible, focusing on communication.
D) I crave emotional intensity and passion in my relationships.
E) I am protective and show my love through action.
F) I express love through dedication and acts of service.
G) I value deep emotional connection but can be possessive at times.
H) I seek a profound emotional bond but may struggle with opening up.

3. What drives your ambition or career path?

A) Achieving control, power, and responsibility over others.
B) Pursuit of knowledge, clarity, and intellectual mastery.
C) Opportunities to network, communicate, and adapt to new situations.
D) Creative freedom and the ability to express my emotions fully.
E) The challenge of overcoming obstacles and fighting for

my goals.

F) The satisfaction of creating and perfecting something with my own hands.

G) Managing emotional challenges and thriving in unpredictable environments.

H) Deep personal transformation and understanding the unseen aspects of life.

4. How do you typically react to conflict?

A) I try to establish order and use my authority to resolve the issue.

B) I analyze the situation logically to find the best solution.

C) I mediate between different parties, finding common ground.

D) I confront emotions head-on and express how I feel without holding back.

E) I don't hesitate to jump into the fight if needed.

F) I step back to solve the problem calmly and methodically.

G) My emotions might flare up, but I work to regain control.

H) I tend to withdraw and reflect before deciding how to respond.

5. What role does creativity play in your life?

A) I use creativity to inspire and lead others.
B) I channel creativity through intellectual pursuits and problem-solving.
C) Creativity is essential for me, and I express it through communication.
D) It's at the core of who I am; I thrive on emotional and artistic expression.
E) Creativity helps me come up with strategies to overcome challenges.
F) I express creativity through my craft, building or making things.
G) I channel my emotions into creative solutions when needed.
H) My creativity comes from deep introspection and understanding life's mysteries.

Results:

Now, count the answers you selected for each letter:

Mostly A: You resonate most with **Zeus** (The King) – Leadership, power, and control.

Mostly B: You resonate most with **Apollo** (The Intellectual) – Logic, clarity, and rationality.

Mostly C: You resonate most with **Hermes** (The Messenger) – Communication, adaptability, and flexibility.

Mostly D: You resonate most with **Dionysus** (The Liberator) – Emotional freedom, spontaneity, and passion.

Mostly E: You resonate most with **Ares** (The Warrior) – Strength, courage, and action.

Mostly F: You resonate most with **Hephaestus** (The Craftsman) – Creativity, skill, and resilience.

Mostly G: You resonate most with **Poseidon** (The Power of the Deep) – Emotional intensity, dominance, and unpredictability.

Mostly H: You resonate most with **Hades** (The Lord of the Underworld) – Mystery, introspection, and transformation.

Chapter 3.

Divine Alchemy. The Dance of Couple's Attractions

Human relationships are a continuous exchange of energies, a meeting of forces that can either harmonize or come into conflict. Archetypes, deeply rooted in the collective unconscious, represent these forces that shape how we relate to others. In the previous chapters, we analyzed the individual male and female archetypes and their impact on the individual. In this chapter, we will focus on how these forces interact within relationships.

When male and female archetypes meet, a dynamic is created that can lead to attraction, collaboration, but also tension and conflict. Each archetype brings not only specific qualities and behaviors but also potential areas of friction. Some combinations can result in a deep connection, such as the meeting of Artemis's independence and Hermes's flexibility, while others, like the relationship between Ares's impulsive force and Hestia's serenity, can be more challenging to manage.

The goal of this chapter is to explore how these archetypal interactions can create balance or imbalance in relationships. However, it is important to note that the concept of balance does not necessarily imply perfect harmony. Relationships often thrive because of the diversity of energies, which offer opportunities for mutual growth. When tensions arise, they can become opportunities to deepen the understanding of oneself and the other.

Unlike the previous chapters, this one is not necessarily meant to be read in a linear fashion from beginning to end. Instead, I encourage readers to explore it actively, identifying their own archetype and comparing it with that of their partner or potential partner. In doing so, it will be possible to better understand how different archetypal energies influence one another and discover new paths toward greater understanding and balance in their relationships.

Reveal the Power of Divine Interactions

Every relationship is a unique dance between archetypal energies—sometimes harmonious, sometimes charged with tension. To truly understand how these forces interact and influence romantic dynamics, we will explore archetypal pairings that generate attraction, create challenges, and offer opportunities for growth. Get ready to uncover how archetypes intertwine, forging deep connections or sparking explosive confrontations.

Compatibility and Dynamics with Male Archetypes:

Aphrodite (The Goddess of Love and Beauty)

Dionysus (The Liberator): This is a relationship that thrives on passion and emotional exploration. Both seek intense experiences and a sensual connection. However, tensions may arise if Aphrodite desires stability while Dionysus continues to seek freedom and adventure.

Zeus (The King): Aphrodite may feel attracted to the power and security that Zeus offers. However, Aphrodite's passionate and free nature could conflict with Zeus's need for control.

Ares (The Warrior): This couple is dominated by physical passion. Their relationship is intense, but Ares's aggression and impulsiveness may lead to emotional conflicts.

Apollo (The Intellectual): While Apollo may admire Aphrodite's beauty, his tendency toward rationality can make him emotionally distant, creating frustration for Aphrodite, who desires a deeper connection.

Hermes (The Messenger): Aphrodite and Hermes may create a relationship based on communication and lightheartedness. However, Hermes's lack of stability may make Aphrodite feel insecure in the long run.

Hephaestus (The Craftsman): Although in mythology Aphrodite is married to Hephaestus, their relationship is often difficult. Hephaestus can provide security and dedication, but his distant nature and focus on work can make Aphrodite feel neglected, leading her to seek comfort elsewhere (as happens with Ares in mythology).

Hades (The Lord of the Underworld): Hades and Aphrodite may form a deep connection based on emotional intensity. However, Hades's introverted nature may make it difficult for him to maintain a dynamic and vibrant relationship, as Aphrodite seeks.

Poseidon (The Power of the Deep): Aphrodite might be attracted to Poseidon's strength and passion, but his turbulent and unpredictable nature could destabilize the harmony and beauty Aphrodite seeks in relationships.

Hera (The Goddess of Marriage and Loyalty)

Zeus (The King): Being archetypally married, this relationship is based on stability and commitment. However, both have a need for control, which can lead to jealousy and power struggles.

Dionysus (The Liberator): Dionysus may be attracted to Hera's stability and strength, but his free-spirited nature could lead to trust issues. Hera, in turn, may feel threatened by Dionysus's lack of commitment.

Ares (The Warrior): Hera may appreciate Ares's strength and courage, but his impulsiveness and tendency to seek conflict may clash with Hera's need for stability.

Apollo (The Intellectual): This relationship could be based on strong mutual admiration. Apollo values Hera's wisdom, and she respects his rationality. However, the relationship may lack the emotional warmth that Hera desires.

Hermes (The Messenger): The relationship between Hera and Hermes could be complex. While Hermes brings flexibility and communication, Hera may find him too unstable and unreliable for her need for stability.

Hephaestus (The Craftsman): Hera may feel safe and protected by Hephaestus, but his emotional detachment and focus on work may not fully satisfy Hera's emotional needs.

Hades (The Lord of the Underworld): Hera and Hades could form a relationship based on deep mutual understanding. Both are strong figures who seek stability, but they may lack passion.

Poseidon (The Power of the Deep):: While Hera might appreciate Poseidon's power, his emotional instability could conflict with her need for control and stability, leading to tension in the relationship.

Artemis (The Goddess of Independence and Nature)

Apollo (The Intellectual): Being siblings in mythology, they share an intellectual and spiritual connection. However, Apollo's tendency to rationalize emotions may frustrate her.

Zeus (The King): Although Zeus respects Artemis's independence, his desire for control may conflict with the absolute freedom Artemis desires.

Ares (The Warrior): Artemis's wild and independent energy may attract Ares. However, Ares's violent tendencies may contrast with Artemis's desire for a peaceful and autonomous life.

Dionysus (The Liberator): Dionysus and Artemis may form an interesting pair, as both are lovers of nature and freedom. However, Dionysus's more emotional nature may clash with Artemis's more detached approach.

Hermes (The Messenger): Hermes could be an ideal partner for Artemis, as he shares her love of freedom and adventure.

However, the lack of emotional grounding might make this couple unstable in the long term.

Hephaestus (The Craftsman): Artemis might appreciate Hephaestus's dedication and patience. However, her need for independence might conflict with Hephaestus's desire for stability and routine.

Hades (The Lord of the Underworld): Hades might be too introspective for Artemis's active energy, as she seeks to stay connected to nature and action.

Poseidon (The Power of the Deep): Poseidon might find Artemis's independence intriguing, but his emotional unpredictability could clash with Artemis's desire for peace and autonomy.

Demeter (The Nurturing Mother)

Zeus (The King): Demeter and Zeus, as in Greek mythology, share a relationship built on power and familial authority. However, Zeus may be too distant and focused on control, while Demeter seeks a more nurturing and emotional bond.

Apollo (The Intellectual): Demeter might appreciate Apollo's rational approach, but could feel emotionally neglected. Apollo's focus on intellect may not satisfy her need for warmth and protection.

Ares (The Warrior): Demeter might admire Ares' strength, but his impulsivity and aggression may conflict with her need for stability and protection.

Dionysus (The Liberator): Dionysus might attract Demeter with his connection to nature and sensual pleasure, but his instability could unsettle Demeter, who values consistency and nurturing.

Hermes (The Messenger): Hermes could bring a lightheartedness that Demeter appreciates, but his wandering and unstable nature might clash with her desire for deep roots.

Hephaestus (The Craftsman): Demeter and Hephaestus form a partnership valuing hard work, family, and creation. Both are dedicated to others, though they might suffer from a lack of direct emotional expression.

Hades (The Lord of the Underworld): Hades could attract Demeter with his depth and introspection, but his dominion over darkness might be too distant from Demeter's protective and nurturing nature.

Poseidon (The Power of the Deep): Demeter could share a connection with Poseidon through their link to nature and fertility. However, Poseidon's strong emotions might unsettle Demeter's need for security and nurturing.

Hestia (The Goddess of Hearth and Home)

Zeus (The King): Hestia's calming, grounding presence could balance Zeus's need for control and power. While Zeus may appreciate her focus on stability, Hestia's preference for peace and quiet could conflict with his authoritative nature.

Apollo (The Intellectual): Hestia and Apollo might form a peaceful intellectual connection. Apollo may admire Hestia's serene, composed nature, but Hestia's focus on home and stability may contrast with Apollo's pursuit of knowledge and external accomplishments.

Ares (The Warrior): Hestia's calm and peaceful demeanor would likely be at odds with Ares's impulsive and aggressive nature. Ares may find her too passive, while Hestia could feel overwhelmed by his intensity.

Dionysus (The Liberator): Hestia and Dionysus may struggle to find common ground. While Hestia values peace, order, and simplicity, Dionysus thrives on chaos, emotional freedom, and indulgence. Their differences could lead to tension, as Hestia might find Dionysus too disruptive.

Hermes (The Messenger): Hermes's flexibility and constant movement could unsettle Hestia's need for stability and routine. While Hermes might enjoy the warmth of Hestia's home, his restlessness and frequent travels could make it hard for them to establish a long-lasting emotional connection.

Hephaestus (The Craftsman): Hephaestus and Hestia could form a harmonious and stable relationship. Both value hard work, dedication, and a focus on building and maintaining stability. Their shared appreciation for craftsmanship and home life could make them compatible, though the relationship might lack excitement.

Hades (The Lord of the Underworld): Hades's deep introspection and Hestia's calm presence could create a balanced relationship. While Hades focuses on the hidden and darker aspects of life, Hestia brings warmth and grounding, helping to temper his more intense nature.

Poseidon (The Power of the Deep): Hestia could find Poseidon's emotional turbulence unsettling, as she values peace and stability. Poseidon's unpredictability might undermine the calm Hestia seeks in her domestic life.

Persephone (The Queen of the Underworld)

Zeus (The King): Zeus may attempt to control Persephone, but her dual nature—between light and darkness—might be difficult to manage. Persephone may seek deeper intimacy than Zeus provides through his external power.

Apollo (The Intellectual): Apollo may appreciate Persephone's ability to navigate both the shadow and light, but his rationality may clash with Persephone's mysterious and emotional depth.

Ares (The Warrior): Ares' emotional intensity might attract Persephone, but his impulsiveness could destabilize her desire for balance between worlds.

Dionysus (The Liberator): Dionysus and Persephone might form a fascinating couple, exploring the extremes of life and death together, though they may struggle to find common stability.

Hermes (The Messenger): Hermes holds a special relationship with Persephone in mythology as a guide between worlds. Their connection could be rooted in deep communication and mutual understanding, though it may lack romantic intensity.

Hephaestus (The Craftsman): Persephone may appreciate Hephaestus' stability and dedication, but she may yearn for more emotional and transformative connection than Hephaestus can provide.

Poseidon (The Power of the Deep): Persephone might be drawn to Poseidon's emotional intensity, but his unpredictability could disturb the balance she seeks between light and darkness.

Hecate (The Goddess of Magic and Crossroads)

Zeus (The King): Hecate might be intrigued by the strength and security that Zeus embodies, but her independence and deep connection to the unknown could create challenges. While Zeus seeks control and order, Hecate thrives in the mysterious and unpredictable realms. This dynamic could lead to a complex relationship where Zeus's desire for structure conflicts with Hecate's preference for freedom and exploration.

Apollo (The Intellectual): Hecate's focus on the mystical and unseen might clash with Apollo's rational, intellectual approach. While Apollo might be fascinated by Hecate's wisdom, her mysterious nature could leave him seeking more logical explanations for her magic.

Ares (The Warrior): Hecate and Ares could form a dynamic, albeit conflicting, relationship. Ares's aggressive nature could clash with Hecate's more strategic and mystical approach. Hecate's power lies in subtlety, while Ares relies on brute force, leading to potential friction.

Dionysus (The Liberator): Hecate and Dionysus could share a mutual appreciation for the darker, more chaotic aspects of life. Both embrace transformation and emotional freedom, though Hecate's introspective nature might be at odds with Dionysus's exuberance and outward expression of emotions.

Hermes (The Messenger): Hermes and Hecate could form a fascinating relationship based on shared communication between worlds. In mythology, they often guide souls and travelers together. While Hermes brings communication and flexibility, Hecate's power over crossroads and magic adds depth to their dynamic. Their connection could be one of mutual respect and complementary skills.

Hephaestus (The Craftsman): Hecate and Hephaestus might not have a natural connection, as their focus is vastly different. Hephaestus's dedication to physical creation and Hecate's focus on magic and the unseen may not align easily, though they could complement each other by blending craftsmanship and mystical insight.

Hades (The Lord of the Underworld): Hades and Hecate could form a deep, transformative relationship. Both are connected to the underworld and to profound change, with Hecate's magic complementing Hades's power over death and the hidden realms. Together, they could explore the deeper mysteries of life, creating a partnership grounded in the unseen.

Poseidon (The Power of the Deep): Hecate may be intrigued by Poseidon's emotional intensity and connection to the mysterious oceans. However, her preference for reflection and strategic control might conflict with Poseidon's unpredictability.

Ariadne (The Guide and Transformer)

Zeus (The King): Ariadne might find protection and power in Zeus, but her independent and transformative nature could conflict with Zeus' need for control.

Apollo (The Intellectual): Ariadne and Apollo could create a relationship based on personal growth and the search for meaning. However, Apollo's focus on logic might be too restrictive for Ariadne's intuitive nature.

Ares (The Warrior): Ariadne could be attracted to Ares' passionate energy, but her need for reflection and transformation could clash with Ares' impulsive and combative nature.

Dionysus (The Liberator): Ariadne and Dionysus form one of the most harmonious couples. Dionysus appreciates Ariadne's ability to guide transformation and embrace life with joy.

Hermes (The Messenger): Ariadne might find in Hermes a partner who helps her navigate life's changes, but his mutable and ungrounded nature could make her feel insecure in the long run.

Hephaestus (The Craftsman): Hephaestus could offer Ariadne stability and support, but his dedication to work might not meet her need for adventure and transformation.

Hades (The Lord of the Underworld): Ariadne could be attracted to Hades' depth and connection to transformation, though his dark nature might be too heavy for her desire to find light through change.

Poseidon (The Power of the Deep): Ariadne might appreciate Poseidon's ability to explore emotional depths, but his changeable nature could disrupt the stability and growth that Ariadne seeks in her transformation.

Athena (The Goddess of Wisdom and Strategy)

Zeus (The King): As Zeus' daughter in mythology, Athena may deeply admire his power, but she may also feel in competition with him for strategic control.

Apollo (The Intellectual): Athena and Apollo could form a relationship based on mutual respect for intelligence and logic. This relationship would likely be balanced and intellectual, though it may lack emotional passion.

Ares (The Warrior): In mythology, Athena and Ares often clash. Though both represent war, Athena is strategic and rational, while Ares is impulsive. This relationship would be marked by constant tension.

Dionysus (The Liberator): Athena might be intrigued by Dionysus' emotional and free-spirited nature, but may also find him too disorganized and chaotic for her need for control and strategy.

Hermes (The Messenger): Athena and Hermes might form an interesting couple based on communication and intellect. Both value mental flexibility, though they may lack emotional depth.

Hephaestus (The Craftsman): In mythology, Hephaestus and Athena often collaborate in creation. Their relationship could be built on cooperation and mutual respect for each other's skills, though it may lack emotional passion.

Hades (The Lord of the Underworld): Athena may appreciate Hades' wisdom, but may find his association with death and darkness too far removed from her logical and strategic approach to life.

Poseidon (The Power of the Deep): Athena and Poseidon often clash in mythology, reflecting their opposing natures: Athena's intellect and strategy versus Poseidon's emotional and instinctive force, creating tension and competition.

Relational Dynamics from the Male Perspective

After exploring relationship dynamics from the perspective of the goddesses, we now shift to analyzing these same relationships from the viewpoint of the male archetypes. This shift in perspective will help us understand how the different gods interact with their female counterparts, delving into the challenges and compatibilities they face as they navigate power, emotions, and control within relationships. Each male archetype engages with feminine energy in its own unique way, revealing new dimensions of attraction, conflict, and growth.

Rather than repeating the analysis for every single god in relation to each goddess, we will instead present a few selected examples that highlight the key dynamics between archetypes. This approach allows us to avoid unnecessary repetition and provides more focused insights into how these archetypal energies intertwine. Readers can apply these reflections to other combinations based on their own experiences and understanding.

Zeus (The King) and Aphrodite: From Zeus's perspective, Aphrodite represents a captivating challenge. He might be attracted to her beauty and passion, but her free-spirited and unpredictable nature could clash with his desire for control. In a relationship, Zeus may try to establish rules to channel Aphrodite's energy, while she could rebel against his need for order. The dynamic between these two archetypes could oscillate between strong attraction and conflict.

Apollo (The Rational) and Demeter: Apollo, the archetype of logic and reason, may admire Demeter's dedication to care and nurturing but could also feel overwhelmed by her emotions. From Apollo's viewpoint, the relationship may become taxing if Demeter constantly seeks emotional reassurance. Apollo might try to maintain emotional distance, preferring a more rational approach to relationship dynamics, which could lead to tensions if they fail to find balance between their differing needs.

Ares (The Warrior) and Artemis: Ares, the god of war, may be drawn to Artemis's strength and independence but also challenged by her refusal to submit or depend on a partner. From Ares's perspective, a relationship with Artemis could be intense and full of passion but also characterized by power struggles and conflicts. While Ares desires a physical connection and a relationship based on strength, Artemis may wish to maintain her autonomy, leading to clashes between the desire for unity and the need for freedom.

Hephaestus (The Blacksmith) and Hestia: Hephaestus, the god of fire and metalwork, might find himself in harmony with Hestia, the goddess of the hearth. From Hephaestus's perspective, Hestia represents the stability and tranquility he seeks after his laborious work. Their relationship would be characterized by harmony and mutual respect, as both share the value of hard work and dedication. However, the challenge for Hephaestus might be keeping the passion alive in a relationship that risks becoming too focused on routine and maintaining domestic security.

Poseidon (The Lord of the Seas) and Persephone: From Poseidon's point of view, Persephone represents a fascinating mix of innocence and hidden power. Poseidon might be attracted to Persephone's duality, spending half of the year as queen of the underworld and the other half as the goddess of spring. However, Poseidon could struggle with accepting her role as ruler of the underworld, as he prefers the emotional dominion and power of the seas over the silent and dark realm Persephone governs with Hades. Their relationship could be marked by deep emotional connection but also conflicts arising from jealousy or a lack of control over Persephone.

Dionysus (The Liberator) and Hecate: Dionysus, god of wine and pleasure, might be intrigued by Hecate's mysterious and occult nature. Both gods are linked to invisible realms: Dionysus to the world of sensory and emotional liberation, and Hecate to the mysteries of the shadow and magic. However, from Dionysus's perspective, their relationship could be a dance between light and darkness. Dionysus might try to pull Hecate out of her isolated and shadowy world, encouraging her to embrace a freer and more fulfilling life, while Hecate might resist, desiring to maintain her control and mystical distance.

Apollo (The Intellectual) and Artemis: From Apollo's point of view, Artemis represents the ideal twin sister, perfectly aligned with his rational nature and sense of justice. Apollo admires Artemis's independence and wild spirit, but may clash with her emotionally distant nature. While Apollo tends to rationalize emotions, Artemis prefers to live away from conventional relationships, which could create tension between Apollo's desire for intellectual understanding and Artemis's need to maintain her autonomy.

Ares (The Warrior) and Aphrodite: From Ares's point of view, Aphrodite is the epitome of passion and carnal love. Ares is drawn to Aphrodite's beauty and sensuality, and their bond is often dominated by intense physical passion. However, Ares may feel frustrated by Aphrodite's free-spirited nature and her desire to be adored by many. Ares's jealousy and his urge to protect what he considers his own could lead to frequent and intense conflicts, as Aphrodite does not want to be bound by any form of possession.

Hermes (The Messenger) and Athena: Hermes, the god of communication and cunning, sees in Athena an intellectually stimulating partner. Their relationship is characterized by a strong mental connection and mutual admiration for logic and strategy. However, Hermes might feel restricted by Athena's seriousness, as she tends to prefer discipline over spontaneity. Hermes, who loves lightness and movement, might try to bring some fun and creativity into their relationship, while Athena may seek to balance this energy with her desire for stability and rationality.

Zeus (The King) and Hera: From Zeus's point of view, Hera represents the ideal queen—strong and worthy to stand by his side in ruling the kingdom. However, Zeus's need to assert his power and personal freedom can conflict with Hera's desire for fidelity and emotional stability. Attracted to many women, Zeus might find Hera's possessiveness stifling, which can lead to tensions. Nonetheless, Hera serves as Zeus's anchor of stability and royalty, even though their relationship is often marked by jealousy and power struggles.

Hephaestus (The Craftsman) and Aphrodite: From Hephaestus's perspective, Aphrodite embodies the beauty and charm that has always seemed unattainable to him. His love for her is deep and devoted, but Hephaestus may feel insecure due to his less attractive physical appearance and reserved nature. While he constantly works to win Aphrodite's love through his craftsmanship and dedication, Aphrodite might feel unfulfilled, seeking passion elsewhere. Hephaestus must confront his shadow of insecurity, accepting that love cannot be earned solely through dedication and work.

Hades (Lord of the Underworld) and Persephone: Hades views Persephone as the queen of the underworld, capable of balancing his darkness with her light. However, Hades is aware of Persephone's desire for freedom and her connection to the world of life and nature. From his perspective, their bond is a fusion of opposites: he represents the stability and permanence of the underworld, while Persephone brings renewing and cyclical energy. This dynamic can create tensions, but also profound transformation, as Persephone helps Hades stay in touch with emotional renewal and rebirth.

Workbook
Balancing Energies Within the Couple

Reflection Questions:

In what situations has your relationship found harmony, and in what situations has it generated tension?

Reflect on the moments of balance and friction in your relationship. Which archetypes might have contributed to these states? Think about specific instances where you felt particularly in sync or in conflict with your partner.

How do you balance your needs with those of your partner?

Relationships require compromise and adjustment. Reflecting on your archetypes, how do you manage the balance between your desire for autonomy, affection, or control and your partner's needs?

What archetypal dynamics do you recognize in your couple's conflicts?

In moments of disagreement or tension, can you identify which archetypal energies are emerging from both sides? How do these energies influence the way conflict is managed? Is it a power struggle, a need for freedom, or a search for stability?

Is there a dynamic that seems to repeat in your past or current relationships?

Reflecting on your past relationships, identify any recurring patterns. Could it be related to a dominant archetype that consistently emerges in you or your partner? How has this archetypal dynamic shaped the course of your relationships?

How can you turn points of tension into opportunities for relational growth?

Consider how your awareness of archetypal dynamics can help you see conflicts not just as obstacles but as opportunities to improve the relationship. How might you reframe these tensions to create more mutual understanding and growth?

Reflection Practice

Take a moment to sit in a quiet space. Visualize yourself and your partner in a moment of conflict or deep connection. Now, observe how your archetypal energies interact, without judgment. Can you identify points where your energies balance or clash? Reflecting on this visualization, how might you cultivate more balance in the relationship?

Chapter 4.

Shadow Work. The Dark Side of Your Archetype

Every archetype contains both light and shadow aspects. While the light side reflects our strengths, virtues, and positive tendencies, the shadow represents the parts of ourselves we tend to repress, deny, or feel uncomfortable with. These shadow traits often emerge in our relationships, creating conflict, distance, or internal struggles.

A particularly fascinating dynamic in shadow work is the way we are drawn to others through our archetypal shadow. In many cases, a man's dominant archetype falls in love with a **feminine archetype** that exists in his own **unconscious shadow**. This means that while his active archetype may guide his behaviors and identity, he is unconsciously seeking balance through a relationship with someone who embodies the repressed or less developed aspects of his own psyche.

For example, a man with a dominant **Zeus archetype** (symbolizing power and control) might unconsciously seek a partner who represents **Aphrodite's archetype** (representing passion, sensuality, and emotional freedom) if these qualities are underdeveloped or repressed within himself. His relationship with the feminine archetype in his shadow may initially feel like deep attraction, but over time, the unresolved shadow traits may create tension or conflict.

This dynamic also works in reverse: a woman might be drawn to a male archetype that represents her own repressed shadow. The archetypes we fall in love with are not random; they often mirror aspects of ourselves we need to confront or integrate. Relationships, then, become a fertile ground for shadow work, where each partner's archetypes are reflected and challenged through the other.

By recognizing how our active archetype falls in love with our shadow's opposite, we can bring greater awareness to our relationships, seeing them not only as sources of love but as opportunities for deep inner work and transformation. Shadow work helps us integrate these hidden aspects of ourselves, allowing us to create more conscious and balanced relationships.

The Hidden Power of Projection

Projection occurs when we unconsciously assign our own repressed qualities—often the traits we deny or feel discomfort with in ourselves—onto another person. In romantic relationships, this can create intense attraction and emotional connection, but it may also lead to conflict if the shadow is not acknowledged.

Projections in Romantic Relationships

When entering relationships, we often project onto our partners the parts of ourselves we haven't fully developed or accepted. Our active archetype consciously shapes our behavior and sense of identity, but the **shadow**—the less integrated aspects—tends to be projected onto the partner, creating both attraction and tension.

For example, someone embodying the **Apollo archetype** (logic, clarity, and perfectionism) might be drawn to a partner who exhibits emotional warmth and spontaneity, traits they might suppress in themselves. This dynamic becomes fertile ground for both growth and conflict. Apollo's partner might feel unsupported emotionally, while Apollo may struggle with accepting vulnerability, highlighting the projection at play.

By recognizing these projections, both partners can begin to integrate the shadow qualities they have been projecting onto each other. This awareness allows for healthier dynamics, reducing conflict rooted in unresolved emotional wounds.

The Mirror Effect in Relationships

Projection works in both directions. Just as one person may project their shadow onto their partner, the partner may project their own unconscious dynamics back, creating a **mirror effect** in relationships. The partner's active and shadow archetypes also come into play, often reflecting unhealed aspects of each other.

For instance, someone with a strong **Artemis archetype** (independence, autonomy) might attract a partner who embodies the **Hermes archetype** (communication and flexibility). While this dynamic may seem complementary at first, over time, Artemis's fear of losing her independence might clash with Hermes's need for constant connection, revealing underlying insecurities in both.

This mirror effect offers opportunities for mutual shadow work. Both partners must recognize their projections and work on integrating the traits they see in each other, rather than expecting the other person to "complete" or compensate for their own shadows.

Wounds and Shadows: The Root of Projections

When we enter into a relationship, the repressed traits of our personality and emotional wounds are closely connected and interact in a complex way. Repressed traits are those parts of ourselves that, due to painful or traumatic experiences, we have learned to hide or deny. These repressions are often a direct response to our emotional wounds. For example, if we experienced rejection as children, we might have repressed our vulnerability and developed an attitude of detachment or self-sufficiency to protect ourselves from the pain of being rejected again.

Emotional wounds—such as abandonment, rejection, humiliation, betrayal, and injustice—therefore create defense mechanisms that influence our behavior. When we repress certain traits because they make us feel vulnerable, they do not disappear but become part of our shadow side. This shadow side is what we project onto others, especially in intimate relationships, where emotional dynamics emerge with greater intensity.

For instance, someone with an abandonment wound might repress their desire for independence and develop an excessive need for reassurance and attention. This person may project onto their partner the responsibility to "fill" that emotional void, making the relationship a fertile ground for tensions and insecurities. Similarly, a person with an injustice wound might repress their emotions and develop a controlling attitude, constantly striving to maintain order and perfection in relationships to avoid feelings of injustice or inequality.

Thus, the shadow sides we project onto others are nothing more than expressions of our unresolved wounds. When we don't work on these wounds, they continue to influence how we choose partners and interact with them. Shadow work, therefore, becomes a key tool to address these wounds, recognize the repressed traits we hide, and bring them to light, allowing us to create more conscious and healthy relationships.

Recognizing our shadow sides inevitably leads to the discovery of the emotional wounds at their root. These wounds, often created in childhood, continue to shape how we relate to the world and our partners.

How Emotional Wounds Develop

Emotional wounds are painful and traumatic experiences that leave deep scars in our psyche. These wounds typically form during childhood, in moments when we experienced emotions of abandonment, rejection, humiliation, betrayal, or injustice—often in response to family or relational dynamics. The lack of tools to manage these emotional experiences leads to the creation of defense mechanisms, which in turn establish behavioral patterns that persist into adulthood.

Emotional wounds, such as abandonment, rejection, humiliation, betrayal, and injustice, are deep scars that impact our psyche. These wounds often develop during childhood, triggered by moments where we experienced strong emotions related to feeling abandoned, rejected, humiliated, betrayed, or treated unfairly, often in response to family or relationship dynamics. The absence of emotional tools to cope with these experiences leads to defense mechanisms that form behavioral patterns, which often persist into adulthood.

However, it's important to note that emotional wounds can form even if we had a happy childhood. This is because it's not just the events themselves but how a child perceives and interprets them that contributes to the formation of these wounds. For example, a child may feel abandoned not because their parents physically left them, but because they perceived an emotional absence or a lack of attention in a crucial moment of need. A parent being busy with work or focusing on another family member could be interpreted as a form of abandonment by the child, even though the parent had no intention of causing emotional harm.

Each child has a unique level of sensitivity and emotional processing, meaning that something an adult views as insignificant—such as a brief moment of inattention or a seemingly harmless comment—might be interpreted by the child as a sign of rejection, abandonment, or injustice. Without the emotional tools to understand or process these feelings, the child may develop defense mechanisms that persist into adulthood, reflecting an unhealed emotional wound.

Thus, emotional wounds aren't exclusively the result of traumatic events; they also stem from subjective perceptions, shaped by the child's sensitivity and interpretation of experiences. These wounds often resurface in adult relationships as fears, insecurities, or destructive patterns, highlighting the need for inner work to heal them.

By recognizing this, we can better understand how shadow work and reflecting on childhood experiences can lead to healing and personal transformation.

The Age of Emotional Wound Formation

Emotional wounds, also known as core wounds, tend to begin forming in early childhood, typically between the ages of 0 and 7. This is a sensitive developmental period when a child is learning about relationships, trust, and their sense of self through interactions with parents, caregivers, and the environment. Children are extremely impressionable during this time, and their emotional responses are shaped by how they perceive events, not necessarily the objective reality of those events.

For example, a seemingly small event like a parent being late to pick up their child from school can be interpreted by the child as abandonment, even if no real abandonment occurred. These perceptions are key because children do not yet have the cognitive or emotional tools to fully understand or rationalize why something happened, which can lead to the formation of emotional wounds like abandonment, rejection, or betrayal. The child's inability to process or make sense of these experiences results in emotional defense mechanisms that can persist into adulthood.

While most emotional wounds begin in early childhood, they can continue to develop and deepen during adolescence, typically around ages 12 to 18. Adolescence is a period of identity formation, increased emotional sensitivity, and the quest for social belonging. Experiences such as bullying, romantic rejections, or perceived injustice from parents or peers can reinforce or introduce new emotional wounds. At this stage, the wounds that may have been more subtle in childhood can become more pronounced as the individual navigates more complex social dynamics and personal identity challenges.

These emotional wounds, whether formed in early childhood or later in adolescence, have a lasting impact on adult behavior, shaping how people relate to others and how they manage emotional conflicts.

Who Has Discussed Them?

The topic of emotional wounds has been explored by various authors, but one of the most well-known contributions comes from **Lise Bourbeau**, author of the book *"The Five Wounds and How to Heal Them"*. Bourbeau explains that these wounds not only affect our relationships with others but also our relationship with ourselves. Wounds generate **masks** that protect us from emotional pain, but in the long run, they prevent us from living fully and authentically.

In addition to Bourbeau, other psychologists and therapists such as **John Bradshaw** and **Alice Miller** have discussed childhood wounds and their impact on relationships. These authors agree that the first step in healing an emotional wound is to recognize it and begin working on its integration.

The Five Wounds in Detail

1. The Wound of Abandonment

The wound of abandonment forms when, during childhood, the child perceives being left alone or neglected by a reference figure. This experience generates a deep sense of insecurity and fear of loneliness. The mask we develop to protect this wound is that of the **dependent**: we tend to constantly seek reassurance and validation from others, fearing being abandoned again.

How it manifests in relationships: A person suffering from this wound tends to be dependent on their partner, constantly demanding attention. This dependency may cause the partner to feel suffocated, creating dynamics of insecurity and jealousy. In archetypes like **Aphrodite** or **Demeter**, this wound manifests as a constant need for reassurance or excessive emotional attachment.

2. The Wound of Rejection

The wound of rejection arises when a child feels unwanted or unloved for who they are. Real or perceived rejection creates a sense of inadequacy and fear of not being accepted. The mask associated with this wound is that of the **fugitive**, as the person tends to avoid confrontations or intimacy for fear of being rejected.

How it manifests in relationships: The fugitive fears emotional intimacy and may sabotage relationships to avoid being rejected. Someone living with the wound of rejection might withdraw from their partner before the partner has the chance to do so. This is seen in the **Artemis** archetype, which tends to maintain emotional distance to protect against rejection.

3. The Wound of Humiliation

The wound of humiliation develops when, during childhood, the child feels diminished or ridiculed, especially by reference figures. This experience creates a deep sense of shame and unworthiness. The mask associated with this wound is that of the **masochist**, as the person tends to devalue themselves or allow others to treat them poorly to avoid further humiliation.

How it manifests in relationships: People with this wound may tolerate abusive or denigrating behavior in relationships, believing they don't deserve better. The **Ares** archetype, for example, can react to the wound of humiliation with outbursts of anger or aggression, hiding the pain behind a mask of strength.

4. The Wound of Betrayal

The wound of betrayal forms when a child feels betrayed by someone they deeply trusted, often a parent. This wound creates a deep mistrust of others and a need to control situations to prevent further betrayals. The mask that develops is that of the **controller**, who tries to prevent any form of deception or infidelity.

How it manifests in relationships: Those suffering from this wound become jealous and possessive, seeking to control their partner to avoid being betrayed. The **Hera** archetype represents this wound well, manifesting in jealousy and attempts to dominate the partner to ensure their loyalty.

5. The Wound of Injustice

The wound of injustice arises from experiences of inequity or unfair treatment, often perceived as excessive rigor or criticism from authoritative figures. The person develops the mask of the **rigid** one, trying to always be perfect and leave no room for emotions, in an attempt to avoid new experiences of injustice.

How it manifests in relationships: Those with this wound tend to be extremely critical of themselves and others, unable to accept imperfection. In the **Apollo** archetype, this manifests as emotional detachment and perfectionism, creating cold and calculated relationships.

The five emotional wounds are fundamental for understanding our behaviors in relationships and in shadow work. Through awareness and the integration of our wounds, we can begin a journey of healing and growth, both personally and relationally. Each archetype reacts differently to these wounds, offering a valuable lens to better understand ourselves and others.

Shadows and Pain: How Divine Energies Reveal Wounds

Each emotional wound manifests differently in the shadow sides of specific archetypes, influencing behavior and relational dynamics. Below, we explore how some of the five core wounds are reflected in certain archetypes, revealing how these wounds shape our actions and relationships:

1. Abandonment

The wound of abandonment often manifests as anxiety and a need for constant attention, leading to manipulative or overprotective behaviors.

Aphrodite (emotional manipulation): When living with the abandonment wound, Aphrodite tends to manipulate those around her to receive constant validation and attention. The fear of being left alone leads her to create emotionally dependent dynamics in relationships.

Demeter (overprotection): Demeter, the nurturing mother, responds to the abandonment wound by becoming overprotective towards her loved ones, fearing abandonment or being left alone. This shadow side drives her to excessively control and protect those she cares for.

2. Rejection

The wound of rejection leads to emotional detachment and isolation, as a defense mechanism to avoid further rejection.

Artemis (emotional isolation): The independence of Artemis reacts to rejection by emotionally closing off. To avoid being rejected, Artemis prefers to distance herself emotionally, choosing independence at the cost of intimacy.

Apollo (detachment): Apollo, who represents logic and clarity, manifests rejection through rational emotional detachment. His wound causes him to avoid confronting vulnerability, hiding his pain behind a cold and distant demeanor.

3. Humiliation

Those who experience the wound of humiliation often react with anger or by completely withdrawing from relationships to avoid exposure.

Ares (aggression): The archetype of Ares, dominated by combative energy, reacts to the wound of humiliation with anger and aggression. His impulsiveness and emotional outbursts serve as a defense against the risk of being diminished or ridiculed.

Hephaestus (withdrawal): Hephaestus, the god of work and creation, tends to withdraw and isolate himself when experiencing the wound of humiliation. He hides behind work and dedication, avoiding emotional contact to protect himself from feeling inadequate or humiliated.

4. Betrayal

The wound of betrayal creates a need for control and jealousy, as the person tries to avoid being betrayed again.

Hera (jealousy): The archetype of Hera is strongly connected to loyalty and commitment. When experiencing the wound of betrayal, she becomes jealous and suspicious, trying to control her partner to prevent potential infidelity.

Dionysus (chaos): Dionysus reacts to the wound of betrayal by creating chaos in relationships. His emotional instability and pursuit of extreme experiences are attempts to escape the fear of being betrayed or deceived.

5. Injustice

The wound of injustice leads to perfectionism and control, as the belief that order and correctness can prevent further suffering.

Zeus (control): Zeus, the archetype of power and command, manifests the wound of injustice through an extreme need for control. He tries to maintain order and justice in relationships, but this leads to tension when he attempts to impose his vision on others.

Athena (perfectionism): Athena, the goddess of wisdom and strategy, expresses the wound of injustice through rigid perfectionism. She strives to be flawless in every aspect, fearing being judged unfairly if she shows any weakness or imperfection.

Emotional wounds manifest in the shadow sides of our archetypes, influencing relational dynamics. Understanding how each wound is connected to specific archetypes helps us recognize our behaviors and begin a healing journey. Shadow work offers us the opportunity to integrate these wounds and improve our relationships, creating a more authentic connection with ourselves and others.

Workbook Exercise: Connecting Your Wound to Your Shadow

In this exercise, you will reflect on your core emotional wound and explore how it connects to your shadow side. This process will help you become more aware of your unconscious patterns and take the first steps toward healing and integration.

Step 1: Identifying Your Core Emotional Wound

Take a moment to reflect on your life experiences. Which of the following emotional wounds resonates most with you? Is it:

Abandonment: Feeling left behind or neglected by someone important in your life?

Rejection: Experiencing a sense of not being wanted or loved for who you are?

Humiliation: Feeling diminished or ridiculed by others, especially those you trust?

Betrayal: Being let down or deceived by someone you counted on?

Injustice: Sensing unfair treatment or lack of recognition?

Write down the emotional wound that feels most relevant to your experiences.

Step 2: Connecting the Wound to Your Shadow

Now, reflect on how this wound influences your behavior, particularly in relationships. Answer the following prompts:

How do I respond when I feel this wound being triggered in a relationship or life situation? (e.g., Do I withdraw, seek control, become defensive, etc.?)

What shadow traits might be present in my response? (e.g., manipulation, overprotection, jealousy, perfectionism, etc.)

Which archetype do these traits align with? (e.g., Afrodite for emotional manipulation, Demeter for overprotection, Zeus for control, etc.)

Write down how your shadow side responds to the wound and which archetype best represents this shadow behavior.

Step 3: Taking Steps Toward Healing

Shadow work is about bringing these unconscious patterns into awareness. Reflect on the following questions to start your healing journey:

What emotions or behaviors do I typically repress or hide when dealing with this wound?

How can I become more aware of these shadow traits when they arise?

```
┌─────────────────────────────────────────────────────────┐
│                                                         │
│                                                         │
└─────────────────────────────────────────────────────────┘
```

What steps can I take to heal this wound? (e.g., seeking vulnerability, setting healthy boundaries, embracing imperfection, etc.)

```
┌─────────────────────────────────────────────────────────┐
│                                                         │
│                                                         │
└─────────────────────────────────────────────────────────┘
```

Write down one actionable step you can take to start healing your wound and integrating your shadow.

```
┌─────────────────────────────────────────────────────────┐
│                                                         │
│                                                         │
└─────────────────────────────────────────────────────────┘
```

Chapter 5.

Evolution of the Inner Divine Through Life's Stages

Throughout our lives, each of us has a dominant archetype that guides our behavior, choices, and worldview. However, it is essential to understand that alongside this dominant archetype, there are also other active archetypes, which may be less visible but equally influential. These secondary archetypes, together with shadow archetypes, form a complex system that represents the multiple dimensions of our personality.

For example, a woman may have **Aphrodite** as her dominant archetype, symbolizing love, beauty, and passion. However, within her, the archetypes of **Hera** (dedication and loyalty in relationships) and **Demeter** (care and protection towards loved ones) may also be active. These secondary archetypes influence her actions, even if they are less prominent than the dominant one. At the same time, other archetypes remain in shadow, meaning they are not fully expressed but may emerge during moments of crisis, transition, or change. One example might be the archetype of **Artemis**, which represents independence and autonomy and could surface during a period of life where the woman feels a need for greater freedom.

It's important to note that our archetypes are not static. Over time, the dominant archetype may give way to a secondary archetype or a shadow archetype in response to new experiences or challenges. For example, a woman who strongly identifies with **Aphrodite** in her youth may, over time, develop a closer connection with **Demeter**, the mother archetype, especially if she steps into a caregiving role within her family.

This archetypal evolution not only reflects individual change but also manifests in relational dynamics. Relationships are not merely the meeting of a masculine and feminine archetype but rather a complex interplay between multiple active and shadow archetypes. For example, two partners may have compatible dominant archetypes, such as **Aphrodite** and **Ares** (physical attraction and passion), but may encounter difficulties due to their secondary or shadow archetypes, such as **Hera** (jealousy and control) and **Dionysus** (chaos and freedom). This interplay of multiple mirrors represents the richness and complexity of human relationships.

In this chapter, we will explore how our archetypes change and evolve over different phases of life, and how these changes influence the way we relate to others and to ourselves. We will discover how the dominant archetype can make room for other archetypes, revealing new dimensions of ourselves and our relationships.

Examples of Inner Transformation

Aphrodite and Demeter: From Passion to Nurturing

In the earlier stages of life, the **Aphrodite** archetype may dominate, focusing on beauty, sensuality, and passion. **Aphrodite** embodies the desire for pleasure, love, and attraction, often linked to youth and romantic exploration. However, as life progresses, there is often a shift toward the **Demeter** archetype, especially when individuals take on roles of caregiving, whether in family, career, or community. **Demeter** represents nurturing, protection, and the need to care for others. The evolution from **Aphrodite** to **Demeter** marks a maturation process where passion may give way to a deeper, more nurturing connection with oneself and others.

Artemis and Persephone: From Independence to Emotional Transformation

The **Artemis** archetype, representing independence and self-sufficiency, often dominates in phases of life where personal freedom and autonomy are priorities. **Artemis** is the archetype of the independent woman, focused on her own goals and values. However, as life unfolds, the **Persephone** archetype can emerge, symbolizing emotional transformation and inner growth. **Persephone** undergoes a journey of descent into the underworld and return, signifying profound emotional shifts. The transition from **Artemis** to **Persephone** involves embracing vulnerability, inner wisdom, and deeper emotional connections.

Zeus and Apollo: From Leadership to Mentorship

Zeus, as the archetype of authority and leadership, is often prominent in the stages of life where power and control are crucial. **Zeus** seeks to dominate, govern, and ensure order. However, with time, there is a natural progression toward the **Apollo** archetype, which embodies clarity, wisdom, and mentorship. **Apollo**, as a mentor figure, shifts the focus from exerting power to guiding others and sharing wisdom. The evolution from **Zeus** to **Apollo** marks the shift from leading to empowering others.

Dionysus and Hermes: From Pleasure-Seeking to Inner Awareness

Dionysus represents spontaneity, pleasure, and the pursuit of emotional freedom. In the early stages of life, there may be a focus on seeking joy, excitement, and living in the moment. However, with age and experience, the **Hermes** archetype often becomes more prominent. **Hermes**, as the messenger and guide, represents communication, flexibility, and inner awareness. The transition from **Dionysus** to **Hermes** involves moving away from external pleasures and focusing on self-knowledge and understanding deeper truths.

Demeter and Hera: From Nurturing to Control, and Vice Versa

The **Demeter** archetype, as the mother figure, focuses on nurturing and caring for others. However, in certain phases of life, the **Hera** archetype may emerge, focusing on loyalty, commitment, and control within relationships, especially in marriage or long-term partnerships. **Hera** seeks stability, order, and fidelity. The interplay between **Demeter** and **Hera** highlights the shifts between nurturing care and a desire for control or structure. At times, **Demeter** may reassert herself in later stages of life, returning to a role of caregiving and emotional support.

The evolution of archetypes reflects the natural shifts that occur as we grow and face new challenges in life. Recognizing how our dominant archetypes change over time allows us to adapt more consciously and embrace the different roles and phases we experience. Each archetype offers unique strengths and lessons, helping us develop a fuller sense of identity and purpose.

Famous Relationships: An Exploration of Divine Dynamics

The relational dynamics between public and famous figures often mirror deeply rooted archetypes, reflecting the energies that shape their unions and challenges.

By analyzing these relationships through the lens of archetypes, we can observe how the dominant forces in each individual have influenced the course of their relationship. In this section, we will explore four famous couples who embody different archetypes at various stages of their union.

Brad Pitt and Angelina Jolie

Initial Phase: Aphrodite and Ares

At the beginning of their relationship, Brad Pitt and Angelina Jolie strongly represented the archetypes of **Aphrodite** and **Ares**. Their union was perceived as intense, passionate, and fueled by physical attraction and chemistry. **Angelina Jolie,** with her image of sensual beauty and rebelliousness, embodied **Aphrodite**, while **Brad Pitt**, with his charismatic charm and strength, could be associated with **Ares**, the warrior. This phase of their relationship was dominated by passion and mutual attraction, typical of these archetypes.

Transition to Demeter and Zeus

Over time, as they became parents, the dynamics between their archetypes began to shift. **Angelina Jolie**, with her role as a devoted mother and her strong commitment to humanitarian work, evolved into **Demeter**, the nurturing mother. **Brad Pitt**, on the other hand, began to assume the role of **Zeus**, the archetype of leadership and authority, seeking to maintain order and structure within the family.

Conflict Between Hera and Dionysus

As the relationship progressed, the archetypes of **Hera** (commitment and control) and **Dionysus** (emotional freedom and chaos) may have begun to emerge. **Angelina Jolie**, taking on the role of **Hera**, may have desired more structure and stability in the relationship, while **Brad Pitt**, embodying **Dionysus**, may have sought greater emotional freedom and self-expression, leading to tension between them.

Final Evolution and Breakup: Aphrodite and Zeus in Conflict

In the later stages of their relationship, the conflict between the desire for power and control (**Zeus**) and the quest for freedom and passion (**Aphrodite**) likely played a critical role. **Angelina Jolie** seemed to return to her **Aphrodite** archetype, rediscovering her independent and passionate nature, while **Brad Pitt**, embodying **Zeus**, attempted to maintain a position of authority and control over the family and the relationship. This dynamic may have contributed to their conflict and eventual breakup.

Archetypes in Evolution

This example shows how dominant archetypes can change over time in a relationship and how these archetypal transitions influence compatibility and dynamics between partners. Brad Pitt and Angelina Jolie, moving from **Aphrodite and Ares** to **Demeter and Zeus**, experienced an archetypal evolution that introduced new tensions and ultimately led to the breakdown of their relationship.

Johnny Depp and Winona Ryder: An Archetypal Perspective

Initial Phase: Dionysus and Persephone

At the beginning of their relationship, **Johnny Depp** could still be seen embodying the archetype of **Dionysus**, representing the rebellious artist, the seeker of emotional and sensory experiences. **Winona Ryder**, with her youthful, ethereal charm, might embody **Persephone**, the archetype of transformation and descent into the unknown. Persephone represents both innocence and depth, moving between light and darkness, much like Ryder's public persona at that time, which alternated between being the darling of Hollywood and being associated with darker, introspective roles.

Intense Attraction: Aphrodite and Dionysus

The intense passion and emotional connection between Depp and Ryder can also be framed within the **Aphrodite and Dionysus** dynamic. Winona Ryder's beauty and allure reflect **Aphrodite**, while Depp's emotional intensity and desire for freedom align with **Dionysus**. Their relationship, while passionate and filled with affection, may have been marked by emotional highs and lows, as is common when these archetypes meet. They are drawn to each other's intensity, but their different emotional needs might create tension, with **Aphrodite** seeking a deeper connection and **Dionysus** resisting emotional constraints.

Breakdown: Dionysus and Hades

As the relationship unraveled, Depp may have transitioned further into his **Hades** archetype, retreating into himself and facing his own inner shadows. **Hades**, as the god of the underworld, is tied to themes of isolation, emotional withdrawal, and personal crisis. This could explain why Depp, after the breakup, described their separation as deeply painful and transformative, even stating that his tattoo, "Winona Forever," was a symbol of the lasting impact she had on him. **Persephone**, Ryder's archetype, naturally complements **Hades**, but in this case, the separation reflects how relationships that draw on deep archetypal forces can leave a profound emotional mark.

Archetypal Evolution Post-Breakup

After their breakup, both Depp and Ryder went through notable transformations. Ryder seemed to embody more of the **Artemis** archetype, focusing on her independence and choosing roles that reflected her inner strength and emotional resilience. Meanwhile, Depp continued to navigate between **Dionysus** and **Hades**, as seen in his career choices and personal struggles. Their relationship, short-lived but intense, reflects the evolution of archetypes in real-life dynamics and highlights how different archetypal energies can influence attraction, conflict, and personal growth.

Archetypes in Transformation

Johnny Depp and Winona Ryder's relationship reflects how powerful archetypes like **Dionysus** and **Persephone** create intense emotional connections. However, as Depp transitioned into his **Hades** archetype, the dynamic shifted, leading to deeper emotional struggles. Their eventual breakup highlights how evolving archetypes influence relationships, with Ryder moving into a more independent **Artemis** role, while Depp continued navigating the complex duality of **Dionysus** and **Hades**.

Marie and Pierre Curie: A Harmonious Archetypal Dynamic

Marie Curie: Athena and Demeter

Marie Curie, known for her intellect, perseverance, and dedication to scientific discovery, embodies a blend of the **Athena** and **Demeter** archetypes. As **Athena**, she represents wisdom, strategic thinking, and intellectual pursuit—qualities that allowed her to break barriers and achieve groundbreaking discoveries in a male-dominated field. Her **Demeter** archetype is seen in her nurturing nature, as she managed to balance being a dedicated mother while contributing significantly to science. Marie's nurturing side also extended to her students, as she later became a mentor to many aspiring scientists.

Pierre Curie: Hermes and Apollo

Pierre Curie could be seen as a mix of the **Hermes** and **Apollo** archetypes. As **Hermes**, the communicator and innovator, Pierre was open to collaboration and was instrumental in the couple's shared discoveries. His intellectual curiosity and adaptability allowed him to explore new ideas with Marie, creating a synergy that pushed their work to new heights. As **Apollo**, Pierre represented clarity of thought, structure, and dedication to knowledge, guiding their scientific endeavors with focus and determination.

The Dynamic: Athena and Hermes, Demeter and Apollo

In their relationship, the **Athena-Hermes** dynamic highlights intellectual collaboration and shared innovation. They worked together on pioneering research, including the discovery of radium and polonium. Marie's strategic mind and Pierre's openness to new ideas created an environment where they could challenge and inspire each other.

On a personal level, the **Demeter-Apollo** dynamic reflects a balanced approach to life. While they were both intensely dedicated to science, they also maintained a harmonious family life, raising two daughters together. Their partnership was marked by mutual respect and admiration, and they complemented each other's strengths and weaknesses, creating a solid foundation both at home and in the laboratory.

The Evolution

As time progressed, their relationship continued to thrive on these core archetypal energies. When Pierre tragically passed away, Marie was deeply affected but continued to build on their shared legacy, embodying even more of the **Athena** archetype as she took on leadership roles in science. Pierre's influence remained a guiding force in her life, symbolizing the lasting impact of their archetypal harmony.

A Model of Intellectual and Emotional Balance

Marie and Pierre Curie's relationship represents the ideal balance between intellectual collaboration and emotional connection. Their complementary archetypal energies of **Athena, Hermes, Demeter,** and **Apollo** created a dynamic that allowed them to succeed not only as a couple but also as scientific pioneers. Their story shows how aligned archetypes can lead to personal fulfillment and professional success, making them a timeless example of a harmonious partnership.

Jean-Paul Sartre and Simone de Beauvoir: A Philosophical Partnership

Simone de Beauvoir: Athena and Hestia

Simone de Beauvoir embodies the archetypes of **Athena** and **Hestia**. As **Athena**, she was fiercely intellectual, driven by her pursuit of knowledge, independence, and wisdom. She was a pioneer in feminist thought, authoring the groundbreaking book *The Second Sex*, where she tackled gender inequality and explored existentialism. However, de Beauvoir also exhibited the quiet, reflective qualities of **Hestia**—the goddess of the hearth—finding solace in her inner world, contemplation, and introspection, which contributed to her philosophical depth.

Jean-Paul Sartre: Hermes and Dionysus

Jean-Paul Sartre, a major figure in existentialist philosophy, can be seen as embodying the **Hermes** and **Dionysus** archetypes. As **Hermes**, Sartre was a communicator, philosopher, and intellectual wanderer, deeply involved in dialogues about freedom, existence, and human nature. His archetypal **Dionysus** energy came from his emotional intensity and desire for rebellion against societal norms, as well as his passionate approach to life and ideas.

The Dynamic: Athena and Hermes, Hestia and Dionysus

In their relationship, the **Athena-Hermes** dynamic was one of intellectual camaraderie and philosophical collaboration. They were both deeply involved in existentialism and worked together, respecting each other's thoughts, without letting conventional romantic expectations interfere. **Simone de Beauvoir's Athena** was drawn to **Sartre's Hermes**, leading them to challenge norms and push boundaries, creating a partnership based on ideas, writing, and mutual understanding.

On a more personal level, **Hestia and Dionysus** created an interesting balance. **De Beauvoir's Hestia**, with her need for independence and inner reflection, balanced Sartre's more chaotic and emotional **Dionysus** side. While Sartre embraced freedom in relationships and exploration, de Beauvoir maintained her centered, reflective nature, allowing both to thrive while holding onto their individual identities.

Archetypal Evolution in Their Relationship

Throughout their lifelong partnership, both Sartre and de Beauvoir remained devoted to their philosophical inquiries. Their relationship evolved from one of romantic partners to more of a shared intellectual journey. Sartre may have transitioned from **Hermes** into more of a **Dionysus**-like figure in his later years, focusing on emotional freedom and rebellion, while de Beauvoir leaned even more deeply into her **Athena** role, championing feminist causes and shaping intellectual history.

Intellectual Collaboration and Personal Freedom

The relationship between **Jean-Paul Sartre** and **Simone de Beauvoir** is an extraordinary example of how archetypes like **Athena, Hermes, Hestia,** and **Dionysus** can coexist in a partnership based on intellectual collaboration and personal freedom. Despite their unconventional romantic arrangements, they maintained an enduring relationship marked by mutual respect, shared growth, and the pursuit of knowledge, proving that harmony can be achieved even in nontraditional ways.

Workbook
Explore Your Divine Dynamics in Couples

The goal of this exercise is to provide a space for deep reflection on your relationship dynamics, helping you better understand how the evolution of your and your partner's archetypes may impact your relationship. By analyzing your relationship through this lens, you can identify areas of conflict and growth, with the intent to create a more conscious and fulfilling connection.

Part 1: Recognizing Your Archetypes

Before beginning, if you haven't yet taken the **test to discover your dominant archetype**, you can find it in **Chapter 1** of this book. It will help you identify the primary feminine or masculine archetype that best reflects your behavior and inclinations.

Which of the following archetypes do you feel has been dominant in your life so far?

(e.g., Athena, Demeter, Hestia, Hermes, Dionysus, etc.)

Describe how this archetype has influenced your decisions, attitudes, and relationships.

```
┌─────────────────────────────────────────────────┐
│                                                 │
│                                                 │
│                                                 │
│                                                 │
└─────────────────────────────────────────────────┘
```

What secondary archetypes do you feel are also active in you?

Reflect on how these secondary archetypes have shaped your behavior and how they may have evolved over time.

```
┌─────────────────────────────────────────────────┐
│                                                 │
│                                                 │
│                                                 │
│                                                 │
│                                                 │
└─────────────────────────────────────────────────┘
```

Part 2: Your Partner's Archetypes

Can you identify the dominant archetype of your partner (or an ex-partner)?

If you find this difficult, consider what behaviors or inclinations may reflect certain archetypes.

Are there aspects of your partner's archetype that create harmony or conflict with your own?

Describe how you complement each other or how your archetypes might be in contrast.

Part 3: Archetypal Evolution in Your Relationship

How do you think your archetypes and those of your partner have changed over time?

Reflect on the changes that have occurred and how the relationship has evolved.

Was there a transitional period when your dominant archetype changed?

Identify what caused this shift and how it impacted the relationship.

Part 4: Final Reflections

How would you evaluate the balance between your primary and secondary archetypes and those of your partner

If you don't feel there is balance, which archetypal energies do you think are missing in the relationship?

What changes would you like to make to facilitate a harmonious evolution of archetypes in your relationship?

Chapter 6.

Shadow Work in Relationships

Once we recognize our emotional wounds, it's easy to fall into the trap of victimhood, transforming this new awareness into a kind of **intellectual ego**. Knowing that we have a wound can become an excuse not to confront it, and our shadows can turn into a fortress behind which we hide. This attitude prevents us from growing, both as individuals and within our relationships. True shadow work, however, requires the courage to let the **masks** fall, to not hide behind the wounds, and to embrace a path of personal and relational growth that is truly authentic.

In today's consumerist society, we are constantly exposed to **false behavioral models**, where relationships are treated like commodities. It becomes easy to jump from one partner to another, avoiding the effort and introspection that a deeper relationship demands. This endless cycle of superficial relationships is the simplest way to avoid the real work on ourselves, as it allows us to bypass the greatest challenge: facing our shadows and fears in a deep and transformative way.

Relationships often follow a cycle of phases: from the initial infatuation, where we idealize our partner, to a later, more mature stage, when the masks fall away. It is precisely then that the real challenge arises: accepting the other for who they truly are and working together to grow as a couple. We must fall in love not only with the light aspects of the other person but also with the archetypes and shadows that make us uncomfortable. If we want the relationship to grow and thrive, we must embrace even what we don't like, both in our partner and in ourselves. However, this is the critical moment: if we want the relationship to evolve, we must **fall in love** not just with the partner's positive traits but also with the shadows that arise, both theirs and our own.

When we choose to **run away** from a relationship, we simply reinforce our **defense mechanisms**. We do nothing but escape from difficulties, avoiding the wounds that the relationship has brought to the surface. Instead, the real challenge lies in staying, in facing those moments of discomfort and conflict, and using them as opportunities to work on ourselves. It's not easy, but it's through this process that we can turn conflict into an opportunity for **growth**, both personally and relationally.

However, it is crucial to recognize our limits. Not all relationships are worth saving, and not all conflicts can be turned into growth. In cases of **dysfunctional or abusive relationships**, where there is physical, emotional, or manipulative violence, it is unhealthy to continue working on the relationship. It's essential to be aware of when internal work becomes an excuse to tolerate abuse or violations of your personal boundaries. In such situations, the healthiest thing to do is to **draw a line** and end the relationship. Shadow work must be done wisely, respecting your individual limits and without crossing personal thresholds "for the love" of the other. True personal growth also requires the strength to **recognize when it's time to let go**.

Conflict as an Opportunity for Growth

Conflicts are often seen as disruptions or breakdowns in relationships, but in reality, they offer powerful opportunities for growth, both individually and as a couple. Viewing conflict from this perspective shifts the focus from "winning" or "losing" to personal development and deeper connection. The key is to approach conflict consciously and see it as a mirror reflecting both partners' emotional wounds and shadow aspects.

1. Embracing Vulnerability

One of the most important elements in transforming conflict into an opportunity for growth is embracing **vulnerability**. Conflicts often bring out insecurities, fears, and shadow traits that we usually try to hide. By being vulnerable during conflict—openly acknowledging our fears and shadow traits—we invite authenticity and emotional intimacy into the relationship. This requires stepping away from ego-driven reactions (like blaming or defending) and instead expressing what we truly feel and need.

For example:

Zeus might struggle with vulnerability because his need for control feels threatened. By admitting to his partner that he fears losing control, he opens the door to greater understanding.

Afrodite, prone to emotional intensity, can learn to express her emotional needs clearly without overwhelming her partner, softening the intensity of her vulnerability.

Being vulnerable is not a sign of weakness but of **strength**, showing that we are willing to be seen fully, even in our imperfect and raw state. Vulnerability encourages both partners to step out of their defensive postures and create space for real connection.

2. Reflection Before Reaction

Conflict often triggers immediate emotional reactions, but these reactions typically come from a place of ego or from unhealed emotional wounds. Before responding to a conflict, it's crucial to **pause** and reflect on the deeper emotions at play. This allows us to respond from a place of conscious awareness, rather than from defensiveness or projection.

An effective tool is to take a **brief pause** during the heat of an argument. Both partners can agree to step back for a few minutes to reflect on their emotional state. This creates room for understanding where each person's emotions are coming from. Are they responding to the present situation, or are they reacting from old wounds (like abandonment, rejection, or betrayal)?

For example:

Apollo, known for his rational approach, might need this pause to shift out of a logical mindset and connect with his emotional side, allowing him to address his partner's feelings instead of focusing solely on solving the problem.

Demeter might need time to understand how her nurturing instinct is being triggered into overprotection or control, rather than responding with unconditional care.

Reflection before reaction allows the **emotional intensity** to settle and opens up space for a more thoughtful and balanced dialogue.

3. Empathy and Compassion

Empathy is the cornerstone of **conflict resolution**. When conflicts arise, it's easy to become self-focused and only consider how the situation affects us. To transform a conflict into growth, we must practice **empathic communication**, which involves putting ourselves in our partner's shoes and attempting to understand their emotional experience.

Each archetype expresses empathy differently, and understanding how each archetype engages with this emotional tool can help:

Dioniso, often driven by intense emotions, might need to temper his emotional reactions by listening more carefully to his partner's needs, making sure he doesn't overwhelm them with his own feelings.

Artemide, fiercely independent, might struggle with empathy because she values her emotional autonomy. She can practice empathy by acknowledging her partner's need for connection, even when she feels the urge to withdraw.

Compassionate communication helps dissolve ego defenses and creates a **safe space** for both partners to explore their emotional wounds without fear of judgment.

4. Turning Conflicts into Learning Opportunities

Instead of viewing conflict as a rupture, it's helpful to reframe it as a **learning opportunity**. Every conflict contains insights into ourselves and our relationship dynamics. Ask yourself: What is this conflict trying to teach me about my needs, my fears, and my shadow? What can I learn about my partner's emotional world through this experience?

For example:

If a **Zeus-Afrodite** relationship experiences conflict around control and freedom, both partners can use the conflict to understand how their respective needs for autonomy and structure are manifesting. Zeus can learn to give Afrodite more emotional space, while Afrodite can learn to express her needs for freedom without disregarding the boundaries of the relationship.

By shifting the mindset from "**this is a problem**" to "**this is an opportunity to grow**", couples can approach conflict with a more open and curious mindset, reducing the fear of confrontation.

Transforming conflict into growth requires vulnerability, reflection, and empathy. Instead of fighting to be "right," both partners can work together to **learn from the conflict** and grow individually and relationally. Every argument is a mirror reflecting back emotional wounds and shadow traits, and by embracing these challenges, couples can deepen their understanding and connection. Through this process, relationships evolve and become a platform for personal and emotional development.

"I" Statements During Conflict

In the context of archetypal dynamics and emotional wounds, the use of **"I" statements** can become a powerful tool for navigating conflict and transforming it into an opportunity for growth. Rather than reacting from a place of defense or projection, **"I" statements** encourage us to communicate from a place of authenticity and vulnerability, directly from our core rather than our defenses. This process not only helps individuals take responsibility for their emotions, but it also fosters an atmosphere of empathy and mutual understanding in the relationship.

When conflict arises, especially between partners embodying different archetypal energies, there is a tendency to project unresolved emotional wounds onto the other person. For example, someone who feels abandoned may accuse their partner of not caring, or someone who feels humiliated may react with anger or aggression. However, by using **"I" statements**, we begin to own our emotional reactions, making it possible to resolve conflicts in a healthier, more constructive way.

"I" Statements in Archetypal Conflicts

1. Afrodite (Fear of Abandonment)

Afrodite's fear of abandonment often manifests in the shadow side as **emotional manipulation**. In moments of conflict, rather than saying, **"You never show me enough attention, you don't care about me,"** which projects the insecurity onto the partner, Afrodite can express her vulnerability in a way that fosters understanding:

"I feel insecure when I don't receive affection, and it makes me feel disconnected from you."

This statement takes responsibility for the emotion and opens a pathway for dialogue rather than accusation.

2. Apollo (Rejection and Emotional Distance)

Apollo's tendency to prioritize logic over emotion can lead to **emotional distance**. In conflict, rather than saying, **"You're too emotional, I can't deal with this,"** Apollo can use an **"I" statement** to express his struggle:

"I feel overwhelmed when emotions are high, and I struggle to stay present because it triggers my need for control."

This reframing helps Apollo acknowledge his discomfort with vulnerability, allowing space for a productive conversation.

3. Ares (Humiliation and Aggression)

Ares, who is often governed by assertiveness, may react aggressively when his shadow is triggered by **humiliation**. Instead of resorting to anger, such as saying, **"You never respect me!"**, Ares can reveal the underlying emotion with:

"I feel disrespected when my opinions are dismissed, and it makes me feel humiliated and want to lash out."

This statement reduces the chance of further aggression by exposing the vulnerable feelings behind the outburst.

4. Hera (Betrayal and Jealousy)

Hera's shadow side, fueled by **jealousy and betrayal**, may provoke her to make statements like, **"You're always flirting with others, you don't value me!"** In such a case, an **"I" statement** can shift the narrative:

"I feel hurt and insecure when I see you giving attention to others, and it triggers my fear of being betrayed." This approach expresses the core emotional wound, creating an opening for a conversation based on empathy rather than accusation.

5. Demetra (Overprotection and Fear of Loss)

Demetra's fear of abandonment leads to **overprotection**. Instead of saying, **"You never prioritize me,"** which puts the partner on the defensive, Demetra can choose:

"I feel afraid when I sense distance between us, and it triggers my fear of being left alone."

This allows her to express her emotional needs without demanding control over the situation.

6. Poseidon (Emotional Turbulence and Control)

Poseidon's archetypal energy is associated with deep emotional undercurrents and sometimes uncontrollable outbursts of anger or frustration. Instead of expressing this emotional storm as: **"You never understand how I feel! You're always ignoring my emotions!"**, Poseidon could frame his feelings through a more reflective and constructive lens:

"I feel overwhelmed when I sense that my emotions are being dismissed, and this makes me react strongly because I fear losing control."

This allows Poseidon to own his emotional intensity while creating space for understanding rather than conflict.

7. Dionysus (Emotional Instability and Freedom)
Dionysus, known for his wild, liberating spirit, might struggle with feeling confined or restricted in relationships. Instead of saying, **"You're always trying to control me and box me in,"**, Dionysus could convey his emotions more openly:

"I feel trapped when I don't have the space to express myself freely, and that makes me anxious and restless." This helps express his need for emotional freedom without attacking the partner, opening a path for dialogue about boundaries and autonomy.

8. Hermes (Communication and Flexibility)

Hermes is the messenger, often thriving in communication and adaptability, but he can also feel misunderstood when communication breaks down. Instead of saying, **"You never listen to what I'm saying!"**, Hermes can frame his frustration through vulnerability:

"I feel unheard when we're not able to communicate openly, and that makes me anxious about where our relationship is heading." This statement opens the door for constructive conversations about communication styles and expectations, without creating a defensive reaction.

9. Zeus (Control and Leadership)

Zeus, often seen as the leader and protector, may feel threatened when he perceives a loss of authority or control. Instead of asserting dominance through phrases like, **"You always try to undermine me!"**, Zeus could express his underlying fears:

"I feel insecure when I think my decisions are being questioned, and that makes me feel like I'm losing my role in the relationship." This shifts the conversation from one of control to one of vulnerability, allowing for more understanding and mutual respect.

10. Hephaestus (Withdrawal and Work Obsession)

Hephaestus may cope with feelings of inadequacy or rejection by immersing himself in work or withdrawing emotionally. Rather than saying, **"You don't appreciate all that I do for us,"**, he could phrase his feelings like this:

"I feel unappreciated when my efforts go unnoticed, and that makes me pull away to protect myself."

By expressing his feelings of rejection more directly, Hephaestus can foster greater emotional connection with his partner.

11. Artemis (Independence and Emotional Distance)

Artemis values her independence and might feel threatened when her space or autonomy is not respected. Instead of saying, **"You're always trying to control me!"**, Artemis could express her feelings like this:

"I feel suffocated when I don't have enough space to be myself, and it makes me worry about losing my independence."

This opens a conversation about respecting personal boundaries without creating conflict.

12. Hestia (Inner Peace and Devotion to Home)

Hestia thrives in creating harmony and a safe emotional environment. She may feel overwhelmed when there's too much emotional disruption. Instead of saying, **"You're always making everything so chaotic!"**, Hestia can frame her concerns more openly:

"I feel unsettled when there's constant tension, and it makes me anxious because I need peace in my environment."

This invites a discussion on creating a more harmonious emotional space without triggering defensiveness.

13. Persephone (Transformation and Depth)

Persephone, being connected with emotional depth and transformation, might feel disconnected when her partner doesn't engage in meaningful emotional conversations. Instead of saying, **"You never talk about anything serious!"**, Persephone could express herself more constructively:

"I feel distant when we don't explore deeper emotions together, and it makes me worry that we're not connecting on a meaningful level."

This opens the door for emotional engagement without pressuring the partner.

14. Ariadne (Emotional Support and Guidance)

Ariadne, as the helper and guide, can feel underappreciated when her emotional efforts are not reciprocated. Instead of saying, **"You never appreciate anything I do for you!"**, she could choose:

"I feel undervalued when my efforts to support you emotionally aren't acknowledged, and it makes me feel disconnected from you."

This allows her to express her need for appreciation in a more open and receptive way.

15. Athena (Wisdom and Strategy)

Athena, who is known for her strategic mind and wisdom, may feel frustrated when her ideas or insights are overlooked. Instead of saying, **"You never listen to my ideas!"**, she can reframe it as:

"I feel dismissed when my perspective isn't taken into account, and it makes me question my role in this relationship."

This opens the conversation to valuing each other's insights and opinions without causing conflict.

16. Hecate (Transitions and Inner Wisdom)

Hecate, being connected with wisdom and life transitions, might feel misunderstood when her need for introspection is ignored. Instead of saying, "**You never give me time to think things through!**", Hecate can express her needs more openly:

"**I feel lost when I don't have the time and space to process changes, and this makes me feel disconnected from myself and the relationship.**"

This encourages her partner to understand her need for reflection without seeing it as avoidance.

17. Hades (Depth and Emotional Intensity)

Hades, as the ruler of the underworld, is associated with deep emotional intensity and introversion. He may feel disconnected when his emotional depth is not acknowledged by his partner. Instead of saying, **"You never understand how deeply I feel things!"**, Hades could express his feelings more vulnerably:

"I feel isolated when my emotional depth isn't understood, and this makes me withdraw even further because I fear my feelings are too much." This statement allows Hades to express his emotional need for understanding without pushing his partner away.

I" Statements in Shadow Work

The **"I" statement** is essential in **shadow work** because it forces us to take ownership of our emotional responses. Often, the parts of ourselves that we project onto others—the parts we have disowned or repressed—are linked to unresolved emotional wounds, as we discussed earlier in the book. These projections manifest in conflict, leading to misunderstandings and perpetuating emotional distance.

By using **"I" statements**, individuals:

- **Take responsibility** for their emotions and reactions.
- **Communicate authentically** from a place of vulnerability, helping to reveal the deeper emotional wounds beneath the surface of the conflict.
- **Invite empathy** from the partner, making it easier to navigate through challenging emotions without escalating into further conflict.

This technique also serves as a pathway to **self-awareness**, as it encourages individuals to reflect on their internal emotional states rather than simply blaming external circumstances or their partners. It is especially helpful in **archetypal conflicts**, where the interplay of different shadow energies can exacerbate emotional tension.

The Cycle of Reconciliation

Reconciliation is not a static endpoint, but a dynamic and ongoing process within relationships. Every conflict, when approached with awareness and openness, can be transformed into an opportunity to explore deeper emotional layers and renew the connection between partners. Shadow work, in this context, is not only about resolving immediate crises but about evolving the relationship itself, fostering greater authenticity and stability. As wounds are healed and shadow aspects are integrated, the couple moves toward a deeper balance, better equipped to face future challenges.

However, this process does not have a definitive conclusion. It is a continuous journey marked by intermediate stages that encourage constant growth. Periods of stagnation or difficulty are not signs of a relationship's end, but rather transitions toward a more mature and conscious connection. Through mutual work on oneself and each other, partners can reach a higher form of love, where imperfections are no longer sources of division but opportunities to grow together, creating an authentic bond grounded in mutual respect and understanding.

Shadow Dialogues: A Practical Exercise

One powerful exercise that can complement the use of **"I" statements** is **Shadow Dialogues**. In this exercise, partners sit down and reflect on a recent conflict, using **"I" statements** to express how their shadow side may have been triggered. Each partner takes turns sharing their feelings without interruption, creating a safe space for both parties to explore how their unresolved wounds influenced the conflict. This practice not only deepens self-awareness but also fosters mutual understanding and growth.

In conclusion, **"I" statements** are a foundational tool for conflict resolution in relationships, especially when engaging in shadow work. They allow individuals to communicate with honesty and vulnerability, transforming conflicts into opportunities for healing and personal growth.

Conclusion.

Embracing Growth Through Archetypes and Shadow Work

Throughout this book, we have explored the transformative power of archetypes and the shadow aspects of our personalities, delving into how they shape our relationships, drive our emotional responses, and reflect our deepest wounds. The journey of self-discovery through these ancient patterns provides a powerful roadmap for understanding not only ourselves but also how we connect with others.

Shadow work has been a central theme, revealing how embracing the darker parts of ourselves, rather than denying them, allows us to grow both individually and as partners. By working through the emotional wounds that often govern our subconscious actions—abandonment, rejection, betrayal, and others—we can transcend limiting patterns and move toward more authentic, meaningful connections.

However, this process of self-awareness and integration is continuous. Just as relationships evolve, so too do the archetypes that guide us. As we mature and face new experiences, our dominant archetypes may shift, allowing us to navigate life with a more comprehensive understanding of who we are. This journey is not linear; it is cyclical, with periods of growth, reconciliation, and deeper connection.

A Journey of Personal and Relational Evolution

By acknowledging both the light and shadow aspects of ourselves, we take the first step toward transforming conflict into growth and challenge into opportunity. The work we do on ourselves ultimately leads to healthier, more balanced relationships—relationships that can stand the test of time, adversity, and change.

As you continue your own journey, remember that this process is ongoing. There is no final destination, but rather a continual evolution of self-awareness, compassion, and love. The more we delve into our archetypal energies and shadow work, the closer we come to living authentically and building deeper, more conscious relationships.

Bibliography

Bolen, Jean Shinoda. *Goddesses in Everywoman: Thirteen Powerful Archetypes in Women's Lives.* Harper & Row, 1984.

Bolen, Jean Shinoda. *Gods in Everyman: Archetypes that Shape Men's Lives.* Harper & Row, 1989.

Bradshaw, John. *Healing the Shame that Binds You.* Health Communications, 1988.

Bourbeau, Lise. *The Five Wounds That Prevent You from Being Yourself.* Éditions ETC Inc., 1994.

Campbell, Joseph. *The Hero with a Thousand Faces.* Pantheon Books, 1949.

Estés, Clarissa Pinkola. *Women Who Run with the Wolves: Myths and Stories of the Wild Woman Archetype.* Ballantine Books, 1992.

Hillman, James. *The Soul's Code: In Search of Character and Calling.* Random House, 1996.

Jung, Carl Gustav. *Archetypes and the Collective Unconscious.* Princeton University Press, 1959.

Moore, Robert, and Douglas Gillette. *King, Warrior, Magician, Lover: Rediscovering the Archetypes of the Mature Masculine.* HarperCollins, 1990.

Van der Kolk, Bessel. *The Body Keeps the Score: Brain, Mind, and Body in the Healing of Trauma.* Viking, 2014.

Mellody, Pia. *Facing Codependence: What It Is, Where It Comes from, How It Sabotages Our Lives.* HarperOne, 1989.